EVERYDAY YOGA

The Essential Guide

Sarah
Dawson

Everyday Yoga – The Essential Guide is also available in accessible formats for people with any degree of visual impairment. The large print edition and eBook (with accessibility features enabled) are available from Need2Know. Please let us know if there are any special features you require and we will do our best to accommodate your needs.

First published in Great Britain in 2011 by
Need2Know
Remus House
Coltsfoot Drive
Peterborough
PE2 9BF
Telephone 01733 898103
Fax 01733 313524
www.need2knowbooks.co.uk

Contents

Introduction

There has never been a greater time to slow down. In the 'noughties' we have tried to achieve more, earn more, and fit more into our days in a culture which has stressed materialistic fulfilment above all else.

This goal of trying to achieve more in order to have more no longer fits our society. Prompted by the credit crunch, the recession, and a period of austerity, people are beginning to re-evaluate what really matters to them. In the process, they are turning away from material gains which were once considered the 'be all and end all' to happiness, and seeking new ways to tackle these challenging times.

More and more people are turning to the ancient science of yoga, a tried and tested method to improve physical and mental health. In the US the yoga industry is said to be growing by over 20 percent a year, and its growth is part of a huge wellness trend.

Over the past ten years yoga has become 'mainstream' in the UK and its popularity is increasing every year. Yoga gives the gift of vitality, wellness and peace of mind, which is a very valuable asset today. While traditional exercise can be aggressive and tough on the body with fast, jerky movements filling muscles with large quantities of lactic acid, causing tiredness and aching -the essence of yoga is balance.

Yoga can tone, lengthen, strengthen and increase flexibility and fitness. Regular yoga practice encourages the ability and opportunity to slow down, to experience gratitude every day, as well as a long-lasting, profound and positive effect on the health.

Contrary to popular belief, yoga isn't dependent on spiritual belief – but it is dependent on practice! Subsequently, *Everyday Yoga – The Essential Guide* aims to introduce practical ways of bringing yoga into your everyday life – however much time you have to spare, and at whatever stage or age you are at.

This book aims to make yoga accessible to all, from the complete beginner, to the more experienced practitioner and invites readers to embrace the system of yoga as a lifestyle, not just a weekly class at the local gym.

In the first few chapters you'll find an overview of yoga, the origins, why it is so beneficial on so many levels, the different forms of yoga and the many styles which have evolved and attracted celebrity followers. In addition you'll find out how to get started with step-by-step approaches to some very basic exercises and breathing techniques which will help promote a good night's sleep or galvanise you into positive action when you have a challenging day ahead.

Ultimately, *Everyday Yoga – The Essential Guide* is an ideal handbook for all the family, from childhood through to senior years, and introduces bite-sized sections of yoga to fit into a busy day.

Whether you're new to yoga and keen to try it out, want to find a way to relax, to enjoy your pregnancy, in your retirement, or a parent or teacher wanting to introduce yoga as playtime or to help with your child's focus, this book will have something for you. Simple diagrams, accompanied by clearly written instructions for safety including resting and anchoring poses to be practised before, after and during a yoga session, guide you through your yoga practice.

Whatever motivates you to practice, remember there are no right or wrong reasons for taking up yoga. As a holistic science, yoga works on all aspects of the self, designed to keep the mind and body alert and healthy so that we can discover our true nature. Once you begin to practice yoga you will embark on a powerful journey of wellness and self discovery.

Acknowledgements

I would like to acknowledge and thank from my heart the many teachers whose classes I have attended over the years and who have inspired me to follow their footsteps and train to become a yoga teacher. In particular, I would like to thank and acknowledge the yoga schools and tutors of the Sivananda and Dru Yoga styles, under which I have trained.

I would also like to thank and acknowledge Francoise Barbira Freedman, a medical anthropologist, author of many international selling yoga/pregnancy books, mother of four, and the founder of the Birthlight Centre who generously shares her wealth of personal and observational expertise in the area of pregnancy yoga in chapter six.

Disclaimer

This book provides information about yoga and its many benefits, but it is not intended to replace professional medical advice, it should always be used in conjunction with conventional medical advice.

The yoga exercises should be followed according to the detailed instructions and diagrams and, if readers are unsure, it is recommended that they attend a yoga class first. Please practice the exercises with care and caution and if you experience any pain, discomfort or dizziness seek medical advice.

In some cases yoga is not advisable. For example, if a person has high blood pressure or incidents of stroke or a heart condition certain asanas, such as the inverted postures and raising arms above the head will need to be avoided. If there is any doubt it is recommended that you consult your GP or take yoga classes with a qualified yoga teacher first.

In ordinary yoga classes it is the student's responsibility to tell the yoga teacher about any health conditions, so that the teacher can suggest appropriate modifications. If you are being treated for any condition, are on medication, and in any doubt about whether you should be doing yoga poses, meditation or pranayama techniques it is recommended that you get confirmation from your GP that it is safe to practise yoga and take note of any movements they advise against.

The writer disclaims any liability of loss in connection with the exercises and advice herein.

! Modifications also need to be made during pregnancy, see chapter six for asana modifications and expert tips from Francoise Barbira Freedman, the founder of Birthlight.

Before You Start

Extra notes

- **!** denotes take care, pay good attention to the instructions and contraindications.

- Allow at least two hours after eating before practising yoga. Do not practise yoga asanas immediately after eating, or when you are hungry.

- Never strain or force your body, learn to recognise and tune into your body's 'limit', the point at which you can stretch to improve strength and flexibility, without causing damage or pain.

- Wear loose, comfortable clothing when doing yoga, tight trousers or tops will restrict movement and make the poses more difficult.

- Yoga asanas are best done with bare feet, so that your feet can connect with the earth and you won't slip when you are doing standing postures, but you can leave socks on during relaxation and in some of the floor work.

- Yoga is all about balance so remember that whatever you do on one side of the body make sure you always do it on the other.

- Your ability and flexibility will vary each time you practice yoga, often dependent on the time of day, or on your general health. Remember that it is a non-competitive form of exercise so learn to foster non self-judgment, allowing your practice to be (or not be) what it is on any given day without criticism.

Resting and anchoring poses

The following positions can be adopted before/after, and/or as resting poses between yoga asanas (exercises) for stillness after movement.

Relaxation (Savasana)

Savasana is best done before and always at the end of any yoga routine. It is also used as a resting position between poses so that the body can integrate the benefits of the previous posture/sequence, and so that 'prana', the life force energy, can circulate around the body.

'Savasana is best done before and always at the end of any yoga routine. It is also used as a resting position between poses so that the body can integrate the benefits of the previous posture/ sequence, and so that "prana", the life force energy, can circulate around the body.'

How

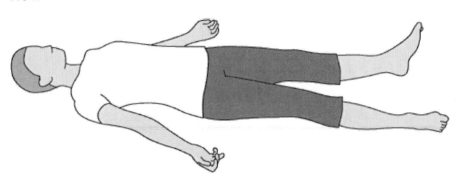

▦ Lie down in a supine position, on the floor, with your legs extended in front of you and your arms by your side. Let your ankles splay wide, and your arms too, opening your hands and facing your palms up towards the sky.

▦ **!** Modification: if your back feels uncomfortable lying flat, bend your knees and bring them together. Place your feet on the floor and slowly tilt up your tailbone, then place it back down on the floor, lengthening the spine and extending your legs back on the mat in front of you, or keeping them bent if necessary.

▦ Relax and breathe evenly in Savasana, on each inhalation feel your lungs expanding and on each exhalation imagine that you are sinking down onto the floor, releasing tension and letting go.

Front-facing Savasana

How

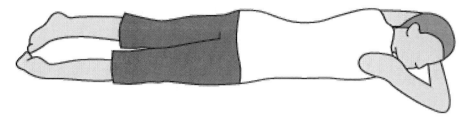

- Similar to classic Savasana, but lying on your front.

- Make a pillow with your arms and turn your face either to the right or left. Let the big toes touch as this relaxes tension in the lower back.

- Feel the contact that your belly makes with the mat. As you breathe in and your tummy presses against the ground all the internal organs are massaged and nourished. Breathe evenly.

- ! Modification: pregnant yogis should take care and modify this asana. Bend your knees, raising them to one side so that you give room for your baby bump.

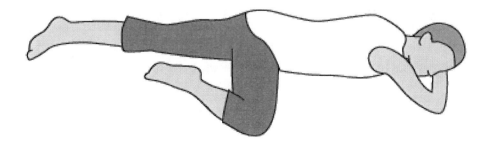

Child's pose (Balasana)

This is a very good asana if you have insomnia, as it stimulates the glands that promote relaxation and sleepiness. Get yourself comfortable in this pose, and simply enjoy the process of breathing and resting. Do whatever you need to do to feel as comfortable as a child, add props such as cushions, a fleecy blanket or a pillow for your forehead, so that you can really let go and enjoy.

How

- Kneel down on the floor so that you are sitting on your heels.

- Push your hips down onto your heels towards the mat. Tip your body and your head down to the floor so that your forehead rests on the mat and your arms are tucked in at the sides, or stretched out in front.

- ! Modification: Complete beginners. Put a yoga block, pillow or make fists with your hands in front to lean your forehead on, as the aim is to drop the hips backwards onto the heels, rather than get the forehead onto the floor.

- Relax your back, breathe evenly and imagine that with each exhalation you are sinking downwards and all the vertebrae of your spine are realigning.

- ! Modification: yogis with back pain or pregnant yogis can widen their knees to release pressure on the lower back or create space for the baby bump.

Supine butterfly pose (Titaliasana)

This is a lovely hip and knee opening posture, great for warming up before going into meditation, sitting cross-legged, or in Lotus position.

How

- Lie on your back in a supine position with legs straight out in front of you then bend your knees and let them fall to the sides, bringing the soles of your feet together.

- Place your arms wide at the side of your body, palms facing upwards. If you would like a stretch in the shoulders/upper back region, take your arms up over the head and gently bring forefingers and thumbs to touch.

- Breathe evenly, give into gravity, and feel yourself supported by the ground.

Lotus, Half Lotus and Easy pose (Padmasana and variations)

These are the three suggested sitting postures for pranayama (yogic breathing exercises) and meditation practice. Begin with Easy pose and when your legs and hips become more flexible try getting into Half Lotus, then in time, when you are more advanced, you could try the full Lotus.

Easy pose (Sukhasana)

How

- Sit on the floor and firstly bend your knees, bring them up towards your chest, with your arms around your knees to lengthen and straighten your spine.

- Release your arms and sit with one leg crossed over the other. Let your knees drop downwards.

- Keep your spine and head straight, face and body relaxed.

- Try changing the order of your legs regularly to keep both sides evenly stretched.

- Relax your hands onto your knees, face down, or bring your thumbs up and forefingers together into the 'chin mudra' hand gesture.

Need2Know

Half Lotus (Ardha Padmasana)

How

- Sit on the floor with your legs out in front of you in a V shape.
- Bend one knee and bring your foot in and place it onto the opposite thigh. Then bring in the other foot, and place it under the opposite thigh.
- Keep your spine and head straight, face and body relaxed.
- Try changing the order of your legs regularly to keep both sides evenly stretched.
- Relax your hands onto your knees, face down, or bring your thumbs up and forefingers together into the 'chin mudra' hand gesture.

Lotus (Padmasana)

How

- Follow the instructions for Half Lotus but lift your second leg in over the first with your foot high on the opposite thigh. Traditional Lotus has the left leg on top.

- Keep your spine and head straight, face and body relaxed.

- Relax your hands onto your knees, facing down, or bring your thumbs and forefingers together into the 'chin mudra' hand gesture.

Mountain pose (Tadasana)

Mountain pose is one of the hardest, yet most beneficial, yoga asanas to achieve. When you have mastered Mountain pose, nothing in life will rock or ruffle your strong inner core, your spine will be in alignment and your tall, confident stance will tell people that you are strong, powerful and peaceful.

How

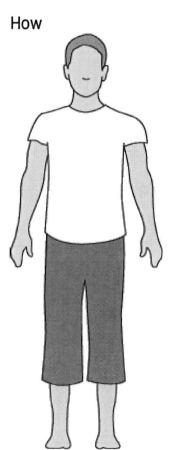

■ Stand on your mat without socks, with your feet parallel and hip-width apart. Think about the contact your feet have with the earth and draw yourself up to full height.

■ Drop your tailbone, tuck your belly inwards towards your spine and imagine you are lifting upwards from the base to the crown of your head.

■ Keep your joints (knees) soft but not bent; relax your shoulders, arms, face and jaw.

■ Scan over different parts of your body – your feet, ankles, knees, thighs, hips, belly, arms, shoulders, neck, head – and visualise yourself growing tall and strong like a mountain.

'Mountain pose is one of the hardest, yet most beneficial, yoga asanas to achieve.

Table pose (Preparation for cat, Marjariasana)

This pose is the starting point for Cat and Cow pose and also for Downward-facing Dog. It is a good position to practise for strengthening your pelvic floor muscles – essential for good posture and a nice toned belly!

How

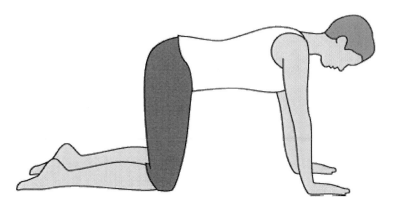

- Kneel on all fours – in the shape of a table top.

- Place your hands directly underneath your shoulders and check that your knees are beneath your hips.

- Flatten the top of your feet onto the mat, placing a cushion underneath the tops of your feet if this is uncomfortable for you, and widen your fingers, stretch out your wrists so that the hands feel 'grounded'.

- Position your pelvis into neutral, letting your belly relax a little downwards then refresh your core muscles, around your abdomen and lower back by drawing your belly inwards slightly and contracting your pelvic floor muscles, then relax your head and neck, keeping them in alignment with the length of the spine.

- Practise this regularly to become familiar with the 'core' muscles.

18

Foetal position

As the name suggests, this is a comfortable, curled-up position, which is adopted when coming out of a lying down posture and into sitting or standing up. As it resembles the foetus in the womb it feels very nurturing.

How

- Lying on the floor, bring your knees up, feet flat on the mat. Let your knees drop over to the right side, away from the heart, and curl yourself up like a baby, breathing evenly.
- Gradually bring yourself into a sitting or kneeling position before moving on with your practice.

Namaste Mudra

A 'Mudra' is a powerful hand gesture which has spiritual and physical benefits. 'Namaste' in Sanskrit translates as hello/goodbye, and is essentially saying 'I salute the light in you'.

When you need peace and quiet and simply to be still, stand in Mountain pose or sit in a comfortable position (kneeling or cross-legged) and bring the palms of your hands together in this peaceful gesture.

How

- Press your palms together firmly and align thumbs and fingers on each hand – bring your elbows wide to the sides.
- Breathe evenly.

Chapter One

What is Yoga and Why Do It?

What does yoga mean?

Yoga literally means 'union', or 'joining', in the language of Sanskrit. It originated some 5,000 years ago in India and was developed to help sages preserve their physical and mental faculties so that they could sit for long hours meditating to achieve self-realisation – this is known as 'enlightenment'.

Since most of us these days are not living solitary lifestyles at the foothills of the Himalayas or wandering the world barefoot as a Sadhu (a spiritual master who has relinquished all material belongings, yet is rich in wisdom) it is unlikely that you have specifically chosen this book with the goal of achieving enlightenment.

However, there are no right or wrong reasons for doing yoga. Some people hope to get a toned, lean body, reduce stress and feel relaxed, prevent ageing, improve posture and reduce back pain, or simply to enjoy the natural 'high' that occurs during and after practice. With a regular routine, and once the very holistic nature of yoga is revealed, you may find yourself open to exploring your spiritual nature even if this wasn't the original intention.

'Some people hope to get a toned, lean body, reduce stress and feel relaxed, prevent ageing, improve posture and reduce back pain, or simply to enjoy the natural 'high' that occurs during and after practice.'

From generation to generation – the lineage process

All the branches of yoga come from an ancient practice developed by sages in India thousands of years ago which was passed down a lineage of teachers to students, in a process known as Parampara. At this time, yoga was only for privileged men who could find a teacher and follow a life of learning from their master.

Yoga arrived in the West around 100 years ago, thanks to many different teachers. Swami Sivananda, and his disciple Swami Vishnu-devananda, were among the first Indian yoga masters to introduce us to yoga, and in 1968 Swami Vishnu-devananda created the first yoga teachers' training course taught in the West.

Sage Patanjali, the original scientist of spirituality, wrote The Yoga Sutras 2,500 years ago, a practical manual which defines the physical and subtle practices of yoga to help the practitioner achieve 'self-realisation' (see next page). The 'yamas' offer a guideline on how to live life in society, for example, non violent behaviour or thinking, and being true, while the 'niyamas' are about your relationship with yourself and how to reach the goal of enlightenment.

By mastering asanas (yoga poses), pranayama (breathing techniques) and dhyana (meditation) the aspiring yogi steadily progress towards the goal of "enlightenment", but be warned, it is likely to take years of commitment and extreme dedication!

Today in the Western world yoga is a booming health industry, popular with both genders, and people of all ages, taught in health centres, gyms, clubs, and corporate environments so that a stressed-out population can become more chilled. Thanks to the many celebrity followers, yoga has become very 'trendy' and there seems no limit to the range of styles to try - from Hip Hop Yoga to Zero Gravity Yoga (performed from a hammock suspended from the ceiling).

Hatha yoga

The main type of yoga known to us today is hatha yoga and this refers to the physical practice of yoga, using the body to control the mind. The word hatha translates to 'ha' meaning sun, and 'tha' meaning moon, because the flow of breath through the right nostril is controlled by the sun and the flow of breath through the left nostril by the moon. Yoga helps to join these two breaths.

Yoga postures are known as 'asanas', which in Sanskrit means 'steady pose'. Asanas revitalise the whole body, principally helping the spine to become more flexible and strong, but also improving the circulation so that nutrients and oxygen can get to the body's cells, massaging the internal organs to keep them healthy, as well as toning all the body's muscles, ligaments and joints.

Hatha yoga is all about balancing the right and left sides of the body (the sun and moon energies), so remember that if you stretch one side of the body, you must always do the same on the other side.

Within hatha yoga there are many teaching styles. Here are a few that you might have heard of:

- Ashtanga.
- Bikram.
- Iyengar.
- Sivananda.
- Kundalini.

Health centres or gyms often describe yoga classes as either hatha or ashtanga to differentiate between a more traditional and slow yoga class (hatha) and a dynamic, athletic style (ashtanga), but as you can see, yoga cannot be defined so simply!

'The postures are known as asanas, which translates from Sanskrit to mean "steady pose".'

The four main branches of yoga

There are many different paths in yoga, but each have the same aim – to bring a person to a higher state of advancement. The ancient teachings define four main branches of yoga (see below) but all paths begin with hatha – the physical practise of yoga.

Raja yoga

This is the systematic analysis and control of the mind, and is considered to be the King of all Yoga. Rather confusingly, raja yoga is also known as ashtanga yoga because there are eight paths and 'ashtanga' means eight in Sanskrit. Ashtanga students will be familiar with the eight 'limbs', or paths, which were compiled by Sage Patanjali, opposite:

Although Raja yoga deals directly with controlling the mind, it also includes the many physical practices of yoga which need 'taming' before you can move up to a higher state.

Jnana yoga

Jnana yoga is the yoga of knowledge, the philosophical approach, using the mind to examine its own nature.

Karma yoga

Karma yoga is the yoga of action or selfless service – doing tasks and work for no personal gain, but simply as an offering to God.

Bhakti yoga

Bhakti yoga is the yoga of devotion, where the yogi aims to channel emotions into devotion through chanting, mantras, ceremonies and rituals to develop humility and channel love to all beings.

Patanjali's Yoga Sutras: The Eight Limbs of Yoga

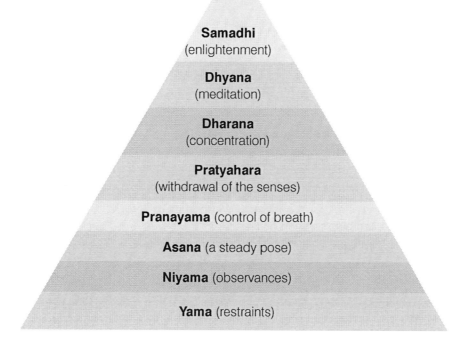

Samadhi
(enlightenment)

Dhyana
(meditation)

Dharana
(concentration)

Pratyahara
(withdrawal of the senses)

Pranayama (control of breath)

Asana (a steady pose)

Niyama (observances)

Yama (restraints)

'When we breathe in, not only are we breathing in life-giving oxygen, but also this powerful, positively charged energy.'

The magic essence of 'prana'

According to yoga philosophy, the universe is filled with a vital life force, or spiritual energy, called prana. When we breathe in, not only are we breathing in life-giving oxygen, but also this powerful, positively charged energy. It is hard to imagine what pranic energy is, but it has been likened to vitamins in food, so you could think of it as vitamin-infused oxygen.

Pranayama is an important element of any yoga practice. 'Prana' means 'life force' or 'vital energy' and 'yama' means 'restraint'. In simple terms, pranayama is about controlling the life force (i.e. your breath) and learning how to use the breath to your advantage to improve your health and wellbeing.

When you have control of prana, you gain control of your breath and then of your mind. Prana is thought to be especially strong at dawn so this is the ideal time to practise pranayama asanas, or meditation.

Chakras and koshas

Chakras are known as energy systems or spirals of energy in the body. There are seven main chakras running from the base of the spine to the top of the head, as well as many smaller ones located around the body, such as in the feet and hands.

Starting at the base is the root chakra, followed by the sacral chakra, then the solar plexus chakra, the heart chakra, throat chakra, the third eye and finally at the top of the head, the crown chakra. All seven chakras are interconnected via a subtle current within the spine.

For balance and harmony in our lives it is important to keep all seven chakras healthy. Yoga can help as each of the asanas directly and positively impacts the chakras, as do meditation and visualisation techniques.

Advanced yogis talk about a vital energy force known as kundalini (a huge force of positive energy which guides you on your path in life). This energy snakes up the spine through each of the chakras until it reaches the crown, at which point the female (Shakti) energy meets the male energy (Shiva), culminating in 'enlightenment' or 'consciousness'. Once kundalini has been released it will depend on a person's dedication as to if, or when, enlightenment is achieved.

The body also has different layers, known as 'koshas', these are:

▧ Anandamaya kosha (our inner 'bliss', our core).

▧ Vijnanamaya kosha (our thoughts).

▧ Manomaya kosha (our emotions).

▧ Pranamaya kosha (the breath).

▧ Annamaya kosha (our physical bodies).

In time you could practise tuning into the other layers for an even deeper yogic experience, with benefits going beyond the physical level of stretching and the breath.

Religious or spiritual beliefs

Before starting yoga, people sometimes wonder whether they will need to change their beliefs or religion in order to practise or benefit from yoga. This is not the case, yoga can be practised by everyone and anyone, from all religions and schools of thought.

Yoga and breathing

Many people breathe shallowly, especially when feeling stressed, fearful or anxious – using only about a third of our lung capacity. This means that very few of us utilise our lungs properly.

The enormous benefits of efficient breathing learned through yoga cannot be underestimated. When you learn to take full yogic breaths you will increase the amount of oxygen, which in turn increases your energy levels and your ability to handle stress will be vastly improved.

Oxygen replenishes all of the organs and helps you tap into your immense stores of energy, this is especially important after a lack of sleep or when stressed. Furthermore, a control of the breath is essential in yoga practice as many of the asanas require deep, steady breathing to get into, stay in, and come out of.

You will learn how to do the full diaphragmatic, or yogic, breath and how to use the breath efficiently for your yoga asanas and during pranayama in the following chapters.

The benefits of yoga

Yoga is completely holistic – it provides an entire health workout, like no other form of exercise around today, bringing so many benefits, on every level: spiritual, emotional, physical and psychological. Yoga was not developed just to achieve a lean and fit body, though this can occur as a result!

Yoga has many great physical benefits. During the sun salutations (see chapter 3) the body gets a good cardiac workout, the inverted asanas, such as Shoulderstand (see chapter 8), work with the force of gravity to send blood from the legs back to the heart, and stretching the muscles forces blood through valves in the veins.

Yoga boosts energy and immunity levels, lowers blood pressure and increases metabolism. All the body's systems get direct stimulation during yoga, in a similar way to receiving acupuncture or shiatsu. Muscle fatigue is counteracted by deep and even breathing and as the physical body is controlled by the nervous and endocrine systems, yoga helps restore balance and harmony.

Achieving calm

'Yoga boosts energy levels, lowers blood pressure, increases metabolism and improves immunity levels.'

Quite often the body gets out of synch when strong emotions arise – whenever we feel angry, stressed, anxious, jealous, sad or insecure these powerful emotions have a negative effect on the body's natural balance.

All feelings are valid but it is how we manage our emotions that is key – for example, if we continually feel stressed in our jobs we may be drawn to over drinking, smoking and late nights; if we feel sad, depressed or anxious this could lead to unhealthy eating habits.

When practising the yoga asanas, breathing exercises and meditation, the nervous system is activated as the body is flooded with nerve impulses. These help the body to rest and repair and results in 'homeostasis' – when all the systems of the body cooperate in an intelligent way and there is complete balance and harmony in the body and mind.

Summing Up

Whatever your reasons for picking up this book, you're now on a journey of self-discovery, learning about how your body responds to yoga, and how your life can positively be impacted through efficient breathing, and other tools and techniques practised by the ancient sages.

It's time to get started. In the next chapter you'll find out how to do so with step-by-step approaches to basic exercises and breathing techniques, whether lying in bed in the morning feeling stressed about your day ahead, or using yoga to help promote a good night's sleep.

Chapter Two
Getting Started

All you need to get started is enthusiasm and a bit of discipline. If you are wondering how to fit some yoga into your busy day-to-day life, how about one of these suggestions:

- If you are someone who hits the snooze button to get an extra 20 minutes in bed, this could be an ideal time to boost your positive energy with some yoga breathing or stretches – while you're still in bed!

- Or, how about swapping the pub some nights with your yoga mat? At the end of a long, tiring day when colleagues invite you for after work drinks, it may seem like you are relaxing but if all you are talking about is work you're not allowing yourself to switch off. Yoga can help you to deeply unwind.

- If your children are keen to play, why not join them and make it yoga time together? That way, you all benefit.

And it's worth knowing that, when you feel most tired, lethargic, unmotivated and lazy, you will quite likely have some of the best quality yoga practices as lethargy is replaced with a renewed sense of energy and peace.

Equipment

You will need some loose, comfortable trousers; jogging bottoms or shorts, and a light top; plus some layers or a shawl to put on for the relaxation at the beginning and end of the session.

You'll also need a yoga mat. To begin with you can use a towel or rug on the floor, but if you plan on continuing yoga then you will need a yoga mat which allows you to place your feet and hands without slipping or sticking and to get in touch with the foot reflexes.

There are many different yoga mats available, including travel mats (which are lightweight and ideal if you travel for work or plan on practising yoga on the go) to thicker versions for extra comfort, which are especially good for asanas which need extra padding, like the shoulder stand where you are resting on your shoulders, or kneeling down.

Finding a class and a teacher

There's a different style of yoga to suit all tastes. If you're interested in fast-paced movements and generating lots of heat then power yoga, ashtanga or Bikram yoga would be best for you. If you prefer moving more precisely or gradually, a class which focuses on correcting alignment and going in and out of asanas mindfully, then Iyengar or hatha yoga might be more suitable.

If you're somewhere in the middle or unsure, why not try out a few different classes and teachers. The style of yoga may be less important than the experience or the connection you feel with the teacher.

Meanwhile, below are some suggestions to help you bring yoga into your daily life. These practices don't necessarily involve going anywhere, costing anything, or making vast changes to your day – these are simple yogic techniques that can be incorporated into any day, at home, on holiday, on a business trip, or when you don't have time to go to a class. Try them and see how they make you feel.

Practice

These simple techniques are your introduction to yoga. They are suitable for everyone, even if you have never done any yoga. Just remember to take note of the ! throughout the book, to ensure it is safe for you to practise.

Wake up Spinal Twist

Why not try this exercise before getting out of bed in the morning, it will help you wake up and feel energised.

How

- Lying on your back in bed, stretch out both legs in front of you with your feet together.

- Raise your hands and interlace your fingers then take them up over your head. Stretch your arms back, and point your toes away from you, then flex your feet towards you to lengthen and wake up the spine, refreshing your entire body. Take a deep breath in and a long exhalation out of your mouth, making a 'sighing' sound to start the day calm and in control.

- Next, bend your knees and place the soles of your feet flat on the bed. Keep your feet parallel and about hip-width apart. Stretch your arms out to each side, at shoulder height, with palms facing upwards, forming a letter 'T' shape

- Take a deep breath in and press your middle back into the mattress. Breathing out, let your knees drop over the right side, turning your face to look over your left shoulder. Breathe evenly, feeling yourself sinking down with each exhalation, enjoying the energising twist in your back.

- Breathe in and bring your knees up to centre, repeating on the other side.

- When you've done each side a few times, take your feet off the bed, bring your knees in towards your chest and hug them, releasing lower back pressure. Then you are ready to start your day, with renewed zest.

! Do not practise twists if you have a back, neck or spine injury.

! Do not practise late at night.

Awakening energising breath

Ever had one of those wonderful days when everything seems to flow effortlessly, you are floating down the stream, rather than fighting against the current? You can help create this kind of day every day by breathing deeply and calmly and bringing yourself into the moment,

Deep diaphragmatic breathing can help you to relax before starting the day. You don't even have to get out of your bed, as it can be done upon waking. Or, if you prefer, you can sit up in Easy pose or Lotus (see Before You Start), placing a pillow underneath your bottom to prevent pressure on the lower back and pelvis.

How

'Deep diaphragmatic breathing can help you to relax before starting the day.'

- Lying on your back, let your body relax, and tune into your breath.

- The full yogic breath has three parts to it. Breathing in, you will feel the movement starting low down in your abdomen as the breath expands your belly then rises upwards, expanding the ribs, finally reaching the shoulders and the collar bone.

- As you breathe out, feel your belly emptying first then the ribs and then the upper chest. When you breathe in, your belly will rise and expand, and when you breathe out, your belly will contract as the lungs empty the stale air.

- To focus the mind, breathe in and count 1-2-3, then breathe out 3-2-1.

- With practice, allow your exhalation to become longer and slower than each inhalation.

Relaxation breathing

If you have to commute to work, you probably don't enjoy it, but if you get a seat on your train or bus this is a great opportunity to fit in some deep breathing and focussed relaxation before arriving at work. This exercise can be done almost anywhere, in a quiet meeting room, and even at your desk if there aren't too many people around, whenever you feel yourself getting stressed or anxious.

How

▓ Uncross your legs, place both feet flat on the ground and get comfortable in your seat. Sit tall – imagine your spine lengthening from the base to the crown of the head, and place your arms loosely by your sides.

▓ Breathe in through your nose as you count to three in your mind, pause for a moment then breathe out of the nose to a count of three. In time, you can increase the length of the exhalation - count to four, five, then six.

▓ Repeat up to six breath cycles.

Visualisation

You can enhance the breathing exercise by visualising a really inspiring and calming place; for example, somewhere you went on holiday or a place you've visited and felt contentment. This is especially beneficial to counter stress and anxiety as it simply switches your focus, and therefore your mood.

How

▓ Picture a scene and imagine you are there experiencing the sights and sounds, the birds, smell of flowers or freshly mown grass, the ocean.

▓ After 5-10 minutes, gently open your eyes and move slowly before continuing with your activities.

▓ Don't worry if you can't think of a scene to use for visualisation - next time you go fo a walk in a park, by the sea, or in the countryside, take photos and use the pictures to jolt your memory and help you recall the sensation of being there.

Seated Spinal Twist

Stop what you are doing for a few moments – especially if you are feeling stressed or tired and make time for a yoga twist. It will help with compressed breathing and it feels good from the inside out as new blood and oxygen flows into the system on the out breath. This exercise can be done anywhere, at work or home, but not while driving or operating machinery!

How

- Keep your feet firmly on the floor, and uncross your legs.

- Take a deep breath in, lifting and lengthening your spine from the base to the crown of the head. Bring your left hand across your right leg and your right arm onto the side of the chair for support.

- With a deep exhalation, slowly begin to twist your body towards the right side. Be careful to feel your spine twisting in stages – from the lower back first, then the middle back, the upper back, and finally the neck and head. Do not force the movement.

- Inhale to return to centre then repeat on the other side.

- Remember, breathe in to lengthen your spine, breathe out to twist around, and breathe in to return to centre.

! Do not practise this pose if you have a back, spine or neck injury. If you have general back ache, go very gently.

Gentle Standing Forward Bend

While you're up from your desk, at lunchtime, in the kitchen making coffee, or in an empty meeting room, a rejuvenating and invigorating back and forward bend will immediately give you a surge of energy and release tension in the back.

How

▪ Stand with your legs about double hip-width apart. Breathing in, place your hands on your hips and expand your chest, drawing shoulders back and down, gently look up at the ceiling, then exhale and bend forwards with a flat back, folding from your hips. Keep your knees soft, and ever so slightly bent.

▪ Relax your head and neck and let your arms hang down, taking hold of the elbows. Breathe evenly, relaxing, hanging down, resting the back. As the blood rushes down to your head it will relax your mind and the entire nervous system.

▪ Come up gradually, with your knees soft, uncurling your spine vertebrae by vertebrae until your head comes up last.

▪ Pause for a few breaths before continuing with your day.

! Be mindful of your neck and back, especially if your back feels tight. Don't overstretch, listen to your body and recognise a good stretch that doesn't cause any pain. Do not try to touch your toes or push yourself down too far. Listen to your body and do only what you feel ready and able to do.

! Do not do this exercise if you have recent or chronic injury to the hips, back or neck.

Yoga before bedtime

Stick to light exercise before going to sleep. Child's pose (Balasana) is ideal for calming the mind and getting you into a relaxed state of sleepiness. Balasana also helps relieve back and neck pain and stretches out the hips, thighs and ankles.

How

'Child's pose (Balasana) is ideal for calming the mind and getting you into a relaxed state of sleepiness.'

▒ Kneeling down, let your knees go wide (or keep them together if you wish, but wide knees is more relaxing for the back), let your big toes touch.

▒ Sink your body and head down towards the bed so that your forehead is resting on the bed and your hips are sinking back towards your heels. You may like to place a thickly folded blanket between your thighs and calves and rest your forehead on a pillow.

! Avoid this pose if you have a knee injury, try Crocodile pose instead. (See chapter seven.)

! Widen knees for pregnancy.

Summing Up

You have now got some ideas on how to incorporate yoga into everyday scenarios and they only take around five minutes of your time. These simple techniques can be done practically any time and anywhere – at home, on a train journey or in bed, and will help to make life more relaxed, flowing and rewarding. Yoga benefits the body as a whole, but as the chapters progress, you will learn which asanas are particularly beneficial for specific conditions or concerns.

Chapter Three

Yoga as a Preventative Medicine

Many people start yoga when a part of their body stops working as well as it used to – for example, back pain, high blood pressure or reduced flexibilty – but if you make it your aim to start yoga when there's nothing actually 'broken', yoga can help you to maintain good health, flexibility and vitality.

Yoga helps to relax the mind and reduce stress levels, it boosts your immunity and energy levels – even when you feel run down, tired or achy, a session of yoga may even override the symptoms. Each asana has been developed to stimulate and nourish all the systems and the organs of the body, helping to keep them in good working order, and alleviate the symptoms of illness.

It is believed that once you master a particular yoga asana, the body goes through a kind of 'rebirth', completely renewing itself.

Benefits

- The yoga asanas restore balance and harmony in the nervous and endocrine systems, they also stimulate, massage and nourish all the organs and systems.

- This leads to a happier, compassionate and calmer mind and, in turn, to better relationships, a happier work/life balance, a more positive attitude, improved sleep, digestion and overall balance.

- The sun salutations give the body a really good cardiac workout, especially when repeated over and over.

'Yoga helps to relax the mind and reduce stress levels, it boosts your immunity and energy levels – even when you feel run down, tired or achy, a session of yoga can often override the symptoms.'

■ Inversion asanas, such as Shoulderstand (see chapter 8) cause gravity to pull blood from the legs back to the heart, which is great for the circulation and anti-ageing.

More than physical

The benefits of the asanas go way beyond the physical. Each asana is associated with an emotion (see chapter 1, Chakras and koshas) and has a corresponding mental thought, for example, when you master Shoulderstand, you are dealing with confidence and communication, performing the Headstand means you have faced your fears about being supported, when you practise the Forward Bend you are 'letting go' of attachments or habits.

Practice

Yoga works as a general preventative medicine to offer good healthy functioning in all the body's systems, organs, glands and muscles. Below is a sequence of asanas which will help prevent (or alleviate) some common conditions today.

Yoga helps to balance your energy so during your practice focus on your body and breath, this will help to quieten your mind, and restore equilibrium. Then allow your practise to enter the other layers, or koshas, noticing which emotions arise, and how each asana makes you feel.

The full sequence below takes approximately 60 minutes but it can be broken down into smaller chunks of time, see the suggestions at the end.

Health-promoting sequence

Savasana

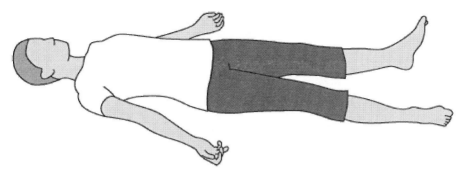

Start in Savasana to fully relax your body. Ideally, spend at least five minutes in relaxation at the beginning and ten minutes at the end. (See variations in Before You Start.)

How

- To begin gently warming up, inhale and raise your right arm all the way over your head, then exhale it back down again. Repeat on the left side.

- Then inhale and raise your right leg, up to a 30-45° degree angle, engaging your abdominal (core) muscles. Exhale and lower it back down. Repeat on the left leg.

- With your arms relaxed at your sides back in Savasana, focus on deep abdominal breathing. On each breath imagine that you are breathing into every cell of your body. With each out breath imagine you are sinking deeper onto your mat, releasing tension and stress.

Supine Spinal Twist

The Spinal Twist is great for the digestion, as it directly stimulates the ascending and descending colons to help keep you regular. It's also really good for increasing flexibility in the spine, and is a great posture to do following Savasana.

How

'The Spinal Twist is great for the digestion, as it directly stimulates the ascending and descending colons to help keep you regular. It's also really good for increasing flexibility in the spine.'

- Bend your knees and bring your heels to your hips so that the soles of your feet are flat on the floor, hip-width apart.

- Stretch your arms out to the sides at shoulder height with palms facing upwards.

- Inhale and tilt up your tailbone very slightly then exhale it back onto the floor. Keeping both feet down, inhale and press the middle of your back onto the floor then breathe out and let both knees drop to the right hand side, turning your face to look over your left shoulder.

- Breathe evenly. Inhale to bring them back up to centre and repeat on the other side. More experienced yogis can enjoy a deeper stretch by taking their feet off the ground before dropping their knees to each side.

- When you've done each side a few times, take your feet off the ground, bring your knees in towards your chest and hug them, releasing lower back pressure.

- The twist can also be performed standing up. (See Senior Yoga.)

! Do not practise twists if you have a back, neck or spine injury.

! Do not practise late at night.

Kapalabhati

Kapalabhati pumps blood and oxygen all around the body and brain, helping to keep the heart, lungs and blood pressure levels healthy. It is considered to be a fairly advanced form of Pranayama (breathing techniques) so if you are new to yoga, less is more to begin with. Huge benefits can be enjoyed when you have mastered this technique but it should never be forced, or hurried. Please take your time.

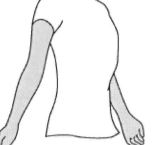

How

 From Savasana or Spinal Twist, let your knees drop all the way over to the right side into foetal position before bringing yourself up into a cross-legged position.

■ Sit comfortably with a straight back, knees crossed either in an Easy pose or in a Half Lotus or Lotus and take two deep breaths in and out. On the third breath in, hold for a beat, then contract and snap in the abdomen on the exhalation. The inhalation is passive so you don't have to think about it, just focus on slowly contracting the abdomen on each exhalation.

■ Start gradually, with just 5-10 gentle pumpings, increasing with time and practice. At first, this may make you feel light-headed so go at your own pace and stop if you feel dizzy.

■ Rest in Savasana afterwards for at least three deep breaths.

! Kapalabhati should not be practised during menstruation, pregnancy, or in the evening due to its very stimulating effects.

'Kapalabhati is one of the six Kriyas (purification practices). It is known as "shining skull" because regular practice elicits a bright, shiny energy.'

1.

Sun salutations – Surya Namaskara

This sequence of 12 carefully designed movements form one of the most highly regarded and frequently practised sequences in yoga.

As its name suggests, you are saluting the sun, the very source of life and vitality, and the energy it provides. If you have time for only one thing, do the sun salutations, as these warm up the entire body. Each one of the 12 movements counteracts the previous one, stretching the body every way, bringing flexibility to your spine and joints and keeping your body slim and limber.

The best time to practice Sun salutations is in the morning.

2.

How

3.

1. Stand in Mountain pose, breathe in and exhale with the palms of your hands together into Namaste Mudra in front of your heart.

2. Inhale and raise both your arms upwards, parallel to your ears and look up at your thumbs. After a few rounds, if you would like more of a backbend, continue inhaling as you open up your chest, push your pelvis forwards and take your arms slightly backwards.

4.

3. Exhale and bring the arms forward first with a straight back, then all the way down to your feet into a standing Forward Bend. Ideally, place your hands on the outside of each foot, aligning fingertips and toes. (You can bend your knees to accommodate this, especially if the backs of your legs feel tight.)

4. Inhale and take your right leg all the way back so that your knee and foot are down on the mat, drop your hips downwards, flatten the top of your foot, lift up and straighten your back to look up. Note: your hands remain in the same place.

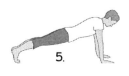

5.

5. Holding the breath, take your left leg back beside your right leg. Come up onto your toes into plank position. Keep your body straight, and your head up, so there is a straight line all along your body. Engage your core muscles.
! Modification: The Child's pose (See Before You Start) is a gentle alternative.

6.

6. Exhale, dropping your knees onto the mat, then lowering your chest and forehead onto the mat, as you do so, your hips remain up – like a caterpillar.

7. With your fingertips in alignment with your shoulders, inhale your head, shoulders

46

and chest up into Cobra pose, looking forwards. (See detailed description in chapter 4.) ! If you have a back or neck injury, do *not* do the Cobra. ! Modification: Front facing Savasana or gradually work towards a Sphinx pose. (Explained in chapter four.)

7.

8. Exhale, tuck your toes under and lift your hips upwards into Downward-facing Dog, an inverted V shape. Press your hands firmly down, keep your head, neck and elbows relaxed with ears parallel to the arms.

8.

9. Take a really big inhalation and bring your right foot forwards, with hands at each side of the foot. Your left leg remains back, with knee and foot flat on the floor. Straighten your back and look up. Initially, beginners can kneel on the opposite leg and help carry the foot forwards with their hands.

9.

10. Exhale and bring your left foot forwards to join your right foot into a forward bend, keeping your hands on either side of your feet, fingertips in alignment with toes, again, bend your knees if you need to.

10.

11. Inhale and lift your spine forwards and up, stretching your arms up to your ears. As with step 2, if you would like more of a backbend, continue inhaling as you open up your chest, push your pelvis slightly forwards and take your arms slightly backwards.

11.

12. Exhale and lower your arms to the side of your thighs. Repeat starting with the left leg. Completion of the two sequences forms a round. Beginners start with one to two rounds, building up with practice.

From Mountain/sun salutations, bend both knees so that you come down onto the mat in a squat position. Place your hands behind you and lie down in Savasana for three to six breath cycles.

12.

! Do not practise the sun salutation sequence if you have a prolapsed disc, or after recent abdominal surgery.

! Avoid position 7, the Cobra, if you have an overactive thyroid, hiatus hernia or peptic ulcer.

! Modifications need to be made during pregnancy, speak to a qualified Yoga for Pregnancy Teacher for advice or see Chapter Six for alternatives.

Forward Bend (Paschimotanasana)

Paschimotanasana boosts physical health, firstly providing a wonderful stretch to the entire back of the body from the neck down to the heels. It massages the liver, kidneys and pancreas, nourishes the digestive system as you bend over your belly, balances the hormones and calms the nervous system.

How .

▨ From Savasana, bend your knees and let them drop over to the right side then gently bring yourself up to a sitting position with your legs straight out in front of you. Sit on a cushion or block if this is more comfortable.

▨ Lengthen from the base of your spine to the crown of your head. Inhale and reach your arms up and over your head then exhale and fold forwards – from the hips, reaching your arms down towards your knees.

▨ Breathe in again and exhale, seeing if you can extend and lower your body down a little more towards your toes. Keep repeating, using the in breath to reach upwards and the out breath to extend and sink downwards – until you feel you have reached your maximum and hold, breathing evenly.

! It is essential to fold from the hips and pelvis, not from the belly and not to round the back. The pose is not about getting as far down as possible, but about lengthening and strengthening the back.

! Do not practise this asana if you have a slipped disc, or sciatica.

! If you have knee/hip problems practise with caution.

Half Locust (Ardha Salabhasana) and Locust (Salabhasana)

The Locust is a back stretch which stimulates all the internal organs, especially the intestines, liver, pancreas and kidneys and is a great reliever of lower back pains. As it is a backbend, it is a stimulating and energising pose.

How

- Turn over to lie on your front to begin with Half Locust. Bring your chin to the floor, stretching it as far forward as comfortably possible.

- Take both arms under your thighs, resting your palms (face down) flat underneath you.

- Inhale and extend your right leg behind you, before raising it, as far as possible without twisting your hips. Exhale and lower, then repeat on the other leg, remembering to keep your chin on the mat and your hips nice and square.

- Experienced yogis can go into Full Locust, following the same instructions but for both legs simultaneously.

- Afterwards, make a pillow with your arms and your face to one side, take 3-6 breaths and relax.

! Do not practise half locust if you have a serious back injury.

! Back bends are stimulating exercises so do not practice these late at night.

'Half Locust is a back stretch which stimulates all the internal organs, especially the intestines, liver, pancreas and kidneys and is a great reliever of lower back pains.'

Eagle (Garudasana)

Eagle is an excellent asana which directly stimulates blood flow in the legs, helping to prevent varicose veins.

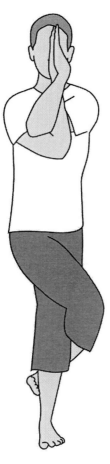

'If you stand or walk a lot for your job then yoga asanas to increase strength in your legs and prevent varicose veins will be very beneficial.'

How

■ Come into Mountain pose, with your feet together.

■ For beginners, take your right leg out to the side. Inhale and cross it over your standing leg (left), so that your knees touch, hold this position for 3-6 breath cycles.

■ For more experienced yogis, cross your knee over the standing leg and wrap your shin around the back. Either hold your arms out wide to balance you, or bring your left arm in front of you, place your right arm over your elbow then bring your arms in together and twist your wrists to place left palm onto right palm.

■ Release your leg and swap sides, bending deeper into the pose with practise.

■ Return to Mountain pose.

! If you have a knee injury, do not practise full Eagle pose, stay in the first position, very gently crossing the legs and coming out of the pose if any discomfort is felt.

Tree (Vrkasana)

The Tree is an excellent posture to alleviate stress, as it helps to stop the chattering monkeys (the ego) and improves concentration and focus. It also builds strength in the legs, relieves back pain.

How

- Start in Mountain pose, focus on putting all the weight into your left leg, then bend your right knee and place your right foot onto the standing leg. Beginners can stand against a wall for support and place the foot on the standing leg's ankle, or on the inner leg, above the knee, while more accomplished yogis can place the foot higher up into the inner thigh of the standing leg or into the Half Lotus.

- Remember to keep your hips straight, with your pelvis facing directly forwards. If you feel you are twisting to one side, lower your foot down your leg to bring your hips square.

- Breathe in and raise your arms to Namaste Mudra, palms together, at the heart or extend your arms upwards, dropping your shoulders back down.

- Breathe evenly while in Tree pose, keeping the standing leg strong and straight, but be careful not to lock the knee joint, keep it soft, but not bent. Hold for as long as comfortable, breathing evenly, then release the leg and change sides.

- Return to Mountain pose and breathe deeply and evenly.

! Keep arms lower down (at the heart in Namaste Mudra) if you have high blood pressure.

'Tree pose is an excellent posture to alleviate stress, as it helps to stop the chattering monkeys (the ego) and improves concentration and focus.'

Triangle (Trikonasana)

Triangle increases peristalsis of the digestive tract and tones the spinal nerves and abdominal organs. It also gives a fantastic lateral stretch to the vertebrae and flexibility to hips and thighs.

How

- Stand with your feet apart and parallel, roughly the length of two times your shoulders. Bring your left foot 90° to your left side and turn your right heel 45° to your right side.

- Inhale, and raise your right arm up towards the ceiling. Exhale and bend the trunk of the body over your left side, turn your head to look up at your right thumb. Your left arm will slide down your leg, towards your foot or you can rest it gently on the front of the knee. Try to keep your hips, your body and your arm in one straight line - practising against a wall can be helpful for this - with the crown of your head as an extension of your spine.

- Inhale deeply, and bend your knee to come out of the pose then change sides. It can be helpful to practise this asana with your back flat against a wall, to ensure you do not lean forwards or backwards with the hips.

! If you have a back, hip or knee injury you should practise Triangle cautiously, coming out of the pose immediately if discomfort or pain is experienced.

! If you have neck pain or high blood pressure, keep your head turned downwards, and keep the raised arm down on your hip if you have a heart condition.

Relaxation (Savasana)

- Finally, lie down in Savasana for 5-10 minutes of relaxation.

- Let your arms rest at the side of your body, palms facing up and tune inwards to your deep abdominal breathing. With each in breath, visualise breathing into all of your body's cells. With each out breath imagine yourself sinking deeper down onto your mat.

- After a few breath cycles, start to consciously relax your body, from your toes upwards, picturing each part of your body softening and relaxing more and more. In your mind, say to yourself 'my right foot is relaxed, my left foot is relaxed, my knees are relaxed', and so on, until you have addressed each part of your body.

- Roll your eyes up under the closed lids, let your lower jaw go slack and relax your tongue in your mouth. Every single muscle will begin to relax and your entire body will feel calm and still.

If you don't have much time

Time is precious, and we don't always have a lot of it to spare, so if you aren't able to fit in this 60-minute practice, take a look at the bite-sized yogic exercises below which allow you to enjoy the benefits – even in a five minute burst.

Practice the following suggestions dependent on your requirements and availability, increasing the amount of time in each pose and during relaxation, when you can. From 30 minutes onwards, your practice will become more 'holistic' with longer-lasting and deeper benefits, especially if done regularly.

Five minutes

Energy re-boot: Savasana + Spinal Twist (lying down, in chair, or standing).

Increase focus/concentration, relieve tension headache and stress: Savasana + Kapalabhati (not recommended in the evening) or Anuloma Viloma (see Chapter 8).

Positive action: One or two rounds of Sun Salutations + Savasana.

Relax, feel grounded: Stand and breathe in Mountain or Tree pose.

Ten minutes

Increase digestive fire/appetite and energy (perform before breakfast): Savasana + Kapalabhati + two rounds of sun salutations + Savasana.

Chill out and unwind (perfect at bedtime): Savasana + Supine Spinal Twist + Forward Bend + Savasana.

Twenty minutes

Cleanse the system (perform before breakfast): Savasana + Kapalabhati + four rounds of sun salutations + Savasana.

Balance and harmony: Savasana + Supine Spinal Twist + Forward Bend + half locust + Tree/Eagle + Savasana.

Thirty minutes

Savasana + Supine Spinal Twist + Kapalabhati + five rounds of sun salutations + Mountain pose + Tree pose + Savasana.

Forty-five minutes

Savasana + Kapalabhati + five round of sun salutations + Mountain pose + Eagle pose + Tree pose + Forward Bend + half locust + Savasana.

Sixty minutes

If you've got a full hour to spare, follow the whole sequence, allowing five minutes at the beginning and 10 minutes at the end for Savasana, and around five rounds of sun salutations.

! In the evenings, do less strenuous postures; two to three rounds of sun salutations, combined with relaxing forward bends, followed by child's pose for its sedative qualities.

! Listen to your body, some days you will feel like doing lots of energetic sun salutations, while others, you may prefer to do gentle floor work on your mat.

Summing Up

You've now got a sequence to practise when you have some spare time in your week. Take it slowly at first, remember that yoga is non-competitive – and that also means not competing with yourself. Recognise that the body feels differently every day, and no yoga practice is ever the same. Some days, you will find an asana relatively easy, on other days you may struggle and feel tight and stiff. This is all part of the process! Some days you will master a balancing pose like Eagle, and other days you might lose all sense of balance. The key is to not be attached to that, and let it be what it is, without self-judgement.

Need2Know

Chapter Four

Yoga for the Back

Yogis say that a person's age is determined by the flexibility of their spine. However, if you don't feel very flexible or sometimes experience back pain, you are not alone. 90% of adults experience some form of back pain in their lives and the NHS say it is the largest cause of work-related absence.

The most common cause of back pain is poor posture, and this can cause deformity and immobility. Doctor's surgeries, chiropractic and osteopathy clinics' waiting rooms are full of people with back complaints, but quite often, all that is needed are some simple exercises to strengthen the core muscles and support the spine.

Standing tall

A healthy spine nourishes the nerves and helps keep the whole body in good health, and a supple back will also help keep the hips, knee and shoulder joints healthy.

Flexibility means you can bend and stretch without too much effort or strain but it decreases with age – especially if we don't exercise. However, felxibility can be maintained, and even attained, with the right kind of exercise done in the right way. Yoga can help relieve tension in the muscles and regular practise of yoga asanas will help prevent back pain by developing good muscle tone and strengthening the abdominal muscles.

'Yogis say that a person's age is determined by the flexibility of their spine.'

As you read this book, take a moment to think about your posture. How are you sitting? If you're sitting with one leg over the other, uncross your legs and place both feet flat on the floor and straighten your back. Imagine a sense of lifting and lengthening from the base of the spine. Breathe in and imagine the breath flowing from the base of the spine up to the top of your head, relaxing and softening all the back muscles and rejuvenating the spine and nervous system. Breathe out; imagine the breath going back down your body releasing tension.

Back awareness

The musculoskeletal system is made up of:

The skeletal system, which is the framework of the body and acts like a shield, protecting all the internal organs.

The joints, which act as hinges and levers and provide mobility.

The muscular system which helps the body to move.

The skeletal system is made up of 206 bones, with ligaments holding everything together. The spine (also known as the backbone) is composed of 33 bones, called vertebrae, which are joined together by cartilage and ligaments. Numbered from top to bottom, these are: Cervical, the vertebrae forming the neck, (C1 to C7), Thoracic, the upper back, (T1-T12), Lumbar, the lower back, (L1-L5) and Sacrum, the tailbone, (S1). The Sacrum is made up of 5 sacral and 4 coccygeal vertebrae which are merged together to form a solid bone - the sacrum and coccyx at the tailbone.

Spaces between the vertebrae are filled with elastic tissue which protects the spine and spinal cord. Unfortunately, these inter-vertebral discs can become compressed by unhealthy movements, and the ligaments (bands of connective tissue) tend to tighten and shorten as we get older. This can apply pressure on the nerves, causing discomfort, and a lack of flexibility.

Spending lots of time sitting slumped over a computer, wearing high heels for long periods of time, an incorrect posture and lack of exercise are all things that will accelerate this. Spinal nerves are connected to virtually all the

'Breathe in and imagine the breath flowing from the base of the spine up to the top of your head, relaxing and softening all the back muscles and rejuvenating the spine and nervous system. Breathe out; imagine the breath going back down your body releasing tension.'

Need2Know

organs in the body via the voluntary and autonomic nervous systems, so it is fundamental for good health that the spine is healthy and our postures well aligned.

Common back problems

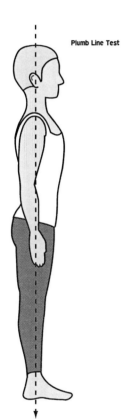

Plumb Line Test

In a healthy adult, the spinal column curves in four parts providing resilience and elasticity. For most people this is not the case, and various conditions can occur in the back such as:

▨ An increase in the thoracic curve (shoulder region) – known as kyphosis. This is someone with hunched or rounded shoulders.

▨ An exaggerated lumbar curve (in the lumbar region, the lower back) – known as lordosis. This is especially common in women and results in a big dip in the lower back, and in extreme cases, a duck-like posture.

▨ A lateral curvature (side twist) – known as scoliosis. This is thought to be caused by poor posture from a very young age.

However, these conditions can be corrected or improved with regular yoga practice and postural/body awareness. Perfect posture exists when someone stands beside a plumb line and the ankles, knees, hips and ears are all in alignment – this is the posture to aim for.

How yoga helps

Many people experience tightness in the hips and shoulders, and lower or upper back pain. The carefully designed forward, back and lateral bends in yoga work on releasing tension, strengthening muscles, ligaments and tendons and on mobilising and gaining flexibility in the back to keep the spine strong and healthy. The body becomes toned, posture improves, core stability muscles grow strong, and thus you appear fitter, taller and leaner and are less likely to have hip, shoulder or knee problems in the future.

'Before attempting to do any of these yoga exercises, it is recommended that you speak to your GP and check that this form of exercise is suitable for you.'

At the end of this chapter you'll find asanas targeted to help with back problems. All yoga styles benefit the spine because the asanas work on increasing flexibility by rotating it forwards, backwards and sideways in a series of twists and bends, but 'gentle' is the key word here. If you are suffering with a weakened back, rather than going for fast paced, advanced or dynamic yoga classes, choose gentle hatha yoga instead and always tell your teacher about your back condition first.

Dru yoga is especially beneficial for relieving back pain, and this style's hallmark is that it is very achievable for all, regardless of age, ability and previous experience. Characterised by flowing movements, performed with soft joints it is a very therapeutic style of yoga with input from osteopaths, doctors, and physiotherapists (see help list).

Since back pain is often linked to stress, you are likely to find the relaxation and breathing techniques of yoga highly beneficial as the more relaxed your mind and body is, the less likely the back will be speaking (or screaming) to you.

Practice

Before attempting to do any of these yoga exercises, it is recommended that you speak to your GP and check that this form of exercise is suitable for you.

Fit the following asanas into your daily practice for a strong, healthy back. Once you become aware of your spine and improve your posture you will look and feel better as the natural flow of serotonin (the feel-good chemical) will be increased, and this will lift your mood.

Even if you only have five minutes, you can do something positive for your back each day, and as the neck muscles connect to the back muscles, stretching the spine in the following ways will also help release neck tension.

Mountain (Tadasana)

When you have mastered the Mountain pose your whole body will be in alignment and your tall, confident stance will tell people that you are strong, powerful and unshakeable. This asana is also described in Before You Start.

How

- Stand on your mat, without socks, and with your feet parallel and hip-width apart. Think about the contact your feet have with the earth and draw yourself up to full height.

- Drop your tailbone, tuck your belly inwards towards your spine and imagine you are lifting upwards from the base to the crown of your head.

- Keep your joints (knees) soft but not bent; relax your shoulders, arms, face and jaw.

- Scan over different parts of your body – your feet, ankles, knees, thighs, hips, belly, arms, shoulders, neck, head – and visualise yourself growing tall and strong like a mountain.

- Initially it can help to use a mirror to check your alignment. In time, you will have no need of the mirror as your body will 'remember' how to be aligned.

Bridge (Setubandasana)

This is a wonderful strengthening exercise for all the muscles in the back (especially the lower back). The Bridge helps to align and increase flexibility in the spine, strengthen and relax the lower back and tight shoulder muscles, tone the abdominal, buttock and thigh muscles.

How

'The Bridge helps to align and increase flexibility in the spine, strengthen and relax the lower back and tight shoulder muscles, tone the abdominal, buttock and thigh muscles.'

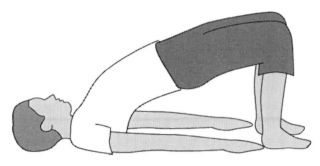

- Lie down on your mat in Savasana, then bend your knees and bring your heels towards your hips, with your feet parallel and roughly hip-width apart, soles flat on the floor.

- Place your hands to the sides of your hips, with palms facing down towards the floor.

- Imagine the vertebrae in your back coming up one by one. Contracting the abdominal and buttock muscles, inhale and lift the tailbone slightly, exhale back down. Inhale again, lifting up slightly higher, and exhale back down. Continue with this flowing movement until you have worked up to resting on your shoulders on an inhalation flowing up through the many levels of the vertebrae. Take your arms wide to the sides but if your neck feels painful, come out of this pose immediately.

62

- Breathe out to lower yourself back down onto the mat, vertebra by vertebra, until finally the tailbone comes back into contact with the mat.

! Always come out of the pose with an out breath and keep the neck relaxed throughout.

! Do not practise this pose if you have whiplash, rheumatoid arthritis or cervical disc problems.

Variations

Try synchronising the movement of raising your hips with raising your hands up over your head so that at the end of the inhalation your arms are right over your head. This gives a wonderful stretch across the front of the body, the abdominal region, the spine and all the muscles in the back.

Once you've practised this asana many times, you can practise staying up and resting in the pose for a few minutes while breathing deeply.

Sphinx

The Sphinx and Cobra postures will strengthen the back muscles, tone the abdominal region and increase flexibility in the spine. Both poses are particularly good for correcting kyphosis and removing the slouch you feel from hours in front of a computer.

The Sphinx is a gentler backbend to the Cobra so try this first and work up to doing the Cobra.

How

'The Sphinx and Cobra postures will strengthen the back muscles, tone the abdominal region and increase flexibility in the spine.'

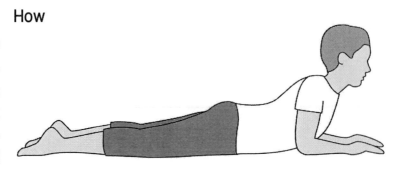

- Lie on your front, with your forehead down on the mat.

- Stretch out your arms in front of you with palms facing down on the floor. Breathe in and bend your elbows out to the sides. Breathe out.

- Then breathe in again, this time pressing down on your hands, lifting up your face and head then straightening your arms so that they are parallel and resting on the mat, at the same time lengthening your spine from the base upwards.

- Keep your elbows directly underneath your shoulders, resembling an Egyptian Sphinx.

- Hold for a few breaths, opening your chest and then slowly come down on an exhalation. Make a pillow with your arms and relax with your face to one side.

Cobra (Bhujangasana)

How

- Lie on your front, with your forehead down on the mat.

- With your arms bent, place your hands beneath your shoulders – fingers just in front of the tops of your shoulders – and keep your elbows close to the sides of your body.

- Taking a deep breath in through the nose, begin to peel your nose and forehead from the mat, gently pressing your hands down onto the mat, begin to slowly curve your spine and raise yourself up like a snake so that your head and chest are lifted.

- Keep your gaze forwards, push down on your hands; keep the elbows soft/ slightly bent and the naval down on the mat, relax the buttocks.

- Breathe out to gently lower yourself back down onto the mat. Take at least three deep breaths before repeating.

! Always uncurl back down to the mat with an out breath.

! Pregnant women should avoid these two postures (see chapter 6 for alternatives).

! This asana should not be practised if you have a peptic ulcer, hernia, an overactive thyroid or back muscle spasms.

! Do not practise Cobra or Sphinx after recent abdominal surgery.

Forward Bend (Paschimotanasana)

The Forward Bend is an excellent asana for boosting physical health and provides an excellent stretch to the entire back of the body from the neck down to the heels, improving flexibility. It is also a recommended corrective asana for lordosis.

How

- Sit on your mat, and adjust your sitting bones so that you are sitting on the flesh of your buttocks, or use a cushion or block if that would be more comfortable. Straighten your legs out in front of you.

- Inhale, reaching your arms up over your head, lengthening from the base of the spine to the crown of your head then exhale and fold forward from your hips, reaching your arms down towards your knees.

- Breathe in again and exhale, seeing if you can extend and lower your body down a little more towards the toes.

- Repeat, using the in breath to reach upwards and the out breath to extend and sink downwards until you feel you have reached your maximum and hold, breathing evenly.

! It is essential to fold from the hips, not from the belly and not to round the back. The pose is not about getting as far down as possible, but about lengthening and strengthening the back.

! Do not practise this asana if you have a slipped disc, or sciatica.

! If you have knee/hip problems practise with caution.

Gentle Supine Spinal Twist

This posture can be practised on a yoga mat, without a yoga mat, on the grass outside, and even in bed. All lateral twists (see also Triangle pose in chapters 3 and 8) are excellent for helping to correct scoliosis.

How

- Lie on your back with your legs straight out on the floor in front of you. Raise your hands and interlace the fingers then take them up over your head. Stretch your arms back, and point your toes away from you, then flex your feet towards you. Enjoy a lovely sense of lengthening, which is waking up the spine and refreshing the entire body.

- Next, bend your knees and place the soles of your feet flat on the mat. Keep your feet parallel and about hip-width apart. Stretch your arms out to each side, at shoulder height, with palms facing upwards.

- Take a deep breath in and let your knees drop over the right side, turning your face to look over your left shoulder. Breathe evenly. Feel yourself sinking down with each out breath and enjoy the twist in your back, which is energising your spine.

- Breathe in and bring your knees up to centre then repeat on the other side.

- When you've done each side a few times, bring your knees in towards your chest and hug your knees to release any lower back pressure.

- The twist can also be performed standing up, see diagram above and instructions on page 126 in Senior Yoga.

! Do not practise twists if you have a back, neck or spine injury. Seek supervision from an experienced teacher.

! Because twists are regenerating, do not do them late at night.

Cat (Marjariasana) and Cow

This flowing movement helps release areas of stiffness and helps to keep your spine healthy and flexible. On the out breath (Cat) you arch the back, and on the in breath (Cow), you create a hollow back. The quality of this asana is in the slowness as this helps you to build awareness of your back and where it feels tight so that you can release it.

How

'This flowing movement helps release areas of stiffness and helps to keep your spine healthy and flexible.'

- Start in Table pose, kneeling on the mat with knees underneath hips and hands underneath your shoulders. Spread your fingers wide and 'ground' your hands..

- Breathe in and breathe out as you engage your core muscles. (See page 18 for full instruction on 'core' awareness and performing the Table pose.) On the exhalation begin to arch your back upwards, moving from the base of your spine, so that you create a dome shape, and eventually tuck your chin into your chest.

- Take a deep breath in and reverse the movement – slowly begin to lower the vertebrae one by one from the base of your spine downwards, as though you are trying to press your belly down onto the mat. As you breathe in, feel each vertebrae moving one by one, until you reach your neck, then lift your neck and head upwards.

- Breathe out, and moving from the base of your spine, begin to arch your back upwards into the dome shape, then inhale and lower it down.

- Repeat three times in each direction.

Need2Know

! Avoid Cat and Cow if you have hiatus hernia.

! If you have wrist or knee problems, repeat the instructions standing up, with soft knees, and hands placed on thighs.

Neck exercises

Gentle movements of the neck are also helpful for alleviating and releasing upper back tension and pain.

How

- Standing in Mountain pose or sitting in a comfortable position with a straight back and neck, look down towards your chest then up towards the ceiling.

- Next, lower your right ear towards your right shoulder, and back up, and then lower your left ear to your left shoulder. Repeat five times on each side.

- Then gently turn your head to look over your right shoulder, back to centre, and then gently turn your head to look over your left shoulder. Repeat five times.

- Use the breath – inhale as you lengthen/extend and exhale as you turn/lower.

Summing Up

You've now got some sequences to help strengthen the back and relieve stiffness or pain. Try to adopt an attitude of consciousness – awareness of your spine and your posture on a day-to-day basis. Focus on standing well in Mountain pose (Tadasana) when waiting at a bus stop or in a queue at the supermarket, with both feet firmly grounded, tailbone tucked in and spine long.

Be aware of your sitting posture. If you work in an office, ask your employer to evaluate your workstation to ensure it is ergonomically sound. Sit with feet flat on ground, and try to avoid crossing your legs as this throws the spine out of synch.

Use the breath to help relieve and relax the muscles, and practise the relaxation and visualisation techniques learnt in chapter 2.

Always check with your GP/back specialist that it is safe for you to practice yoga for your back or do any of these exercises.

Chapter Five

Meditate to Reduce Stress

Our minds today are overloaded by all sorts of stimulation – from traffic to the ping of technology telling us that we have another email, text or missed call to deal with. And then there is social media and its many distractions - from texting to tweeting and installing the latest 'app' our obsession with technology is making it hard to concentrate on one thing at a time and to process data efficiently.

In this chapter we look at how meditation can reduce stress levels, improve concentration and focus, and consequently the quality, peacefulness and enjoyment in life. No matter what is going on 'out there' you will learn to create space in your mind and remain calm, centred and in control, so that you are much better equipped to deal with all the 'busyness' and noise.

What does it mean to meditate?

When the mind is agitated by everyday things it is impossible to feel relaxed. For most of us, the mind jumps from one thought to another, from the past to the future. It is only when we are still that we can connect with the present moment and enjoy the tranquillity that lies within. Meditation helps you achieve this.

When we think of meditation, the image of a spiritual monk sat in the Lotus position chanting 'Om' probably springs to mind. But many of us are engaged in meditation in our daily tasks without really realising it – for a keen gardener, the time spent tending your garden will be devoted to just that, in other words, your passion and interest in gardening is so great that all other thoughts are forgotten. When your thoughts, concentration and focus are on one thing only, this is a form of meditation.

Meditation is a bit like praying, but rather than praying to something or someone, we are getting in touch with an incredible and divine energy that lies within us.

Who should meditate and why?

'By stilling and slowing down our breathing we can learn to quieten the mind and when we do, all cares and worries disappear as we glimpse our true "self".'

Anyone who is feeling overwhelmed, stressed, or worried will benefit enormously from meditation and we are all capable of bringing our minds into a calm and meditative state. By stilling and slowing down our breathing we can learn to slow down our thoughts and when we do, all cares and worries disappear as we glimpse our true 'self'.

The benefits are enormous; the quality of sleep will improve, stress hormones will be reduced as the levels of endorphins (the feel-good hormones) increase, the immune system is boosted and you'll have bundles more energy.

Different types of meditation

There is a range of different meditation practices to try today, from Buddhist meditation (based on the teachings of Buddha) and Vipassana, to the hugely popular Transcendental Meditation, or TM. Founded by yogi, Maharishi Mahesh, TM was popularised by The Beatles in the sixties and described as a 'completely natural, effortless practice'. TM has widespread health benefits and a number of British doctors are petitioning to the government for it to be widely available on the NHS.

Another popular technique which is becoming quite mainstream, being offered in schools and businesses, is 'Mindfulness' which is also based on Buddhist principles. This technique helps people live more in the present moment to find stillness in a stressful world. As with traditional meditation, Mindfulness helps people improve concentration, thinking, creativity and harmony.

As you explore yoga you will discover that it teaches no single method to meditate. For most of us it would probably be a huge relief merely to stop the chattering monkeys for a short period of time each day. So, for simplicity, below are two types of meditation that you could try:

- Saguna meditation concentrates on an object; something with qualities, for example, a symbol, a mantra (like 'Om') or an image (such as the Cross). This type of meditation is 'dualistic' as it means that the person meditating thinks of themselves as separate from the object of focus.

- Nirguna meditation is more abstract, the person meditating concentrates on expanding and merging to become 'one' with the universe, and is therefore non-dualistic.

Create a routine

Routines are good for us as they help give us motivation and discipline, and the best way to learn to meditate is to do it at the same time each day. Choose a time to best suit you but don't get too caught up on perfect conditions – the important thing is to do it!

Yoga philosophy says the ideal time to meditate is dawn or dusk as the air is charged with positive energy or life force, known as 'prana', but if this isn't suitable choose a part of the day that works for you. Start small, with just 10-15 minutes before bedtime, or after arriving home from work. Set a fixed amount of time and gradually increase it.

If possible, dedicate a space or part of a room which will be for the practice of meditation, and set the scene. Place a spiritual or inspirational picture, statue or photograph in the direction that you will be facing, note that it is best to face either the east or north to benefit from the energetic flow in these positions. Some people enjoy burning incense or aromatherapy oils when they meditate, or lighting candles to make it a full sensory experience.

Get comfortable

It is a good idea to do some exercise or relaxation beforehand so that you feel more comfortable to sit in stillness. Ensure you're warm before beginning to meditate, wear loose clothing and put something like a blanket or shawl, over your shoulders as your body temperature will cool down. It is important that you are relaxed, yet alert, the purpose of meditation is not to fall asleep. This is why lying down is not a recommended meditation position.

'Ensure you're warm before beginning to meditate, wear loose clothing and put something like a blanket or shawl, over your shoulders as your body temperature will cool down.'

Sit in a cross-legged Easy pose or Half Lotus or Lotus. This position provides a firm triangular shape to allow the 'prana' to flow, and blocks the energy in the feet and legs so that it can flow up to the third eye chakra, which is associated with intuition and wisdom, and is located between the eyebrows.

Having good posture is very important for meditation. Place a cushion or pillow under your sitting bones so that your lower back is supported and your spine is nice and straight from the base to the crown of the head. Push the pelvis slightly forwards so that all the chakras in the spine are open and in alignment while meditating. Try to avoid dropping your head so that the throat chakra stays open and energy can travel up the spine to the third eye. Equally, push forwards and open your chest to keep your heart area and heart chakra open.

Alternatively, until you become more used to sitting cross-legged, you can sit on a chair for meditation – just ensure your back is upright and your legs/body are relaxed, and that both feet are placed flat on the floor.

Place your hands on top of one another in front of you, or let your index fingers and thumbs lightly touch – this is known as 'Chin Mudra'. As your finger and thumb come together it creates a little circle, which represents 'Om', the oneness of the universe, and it subtly sends a message to the mind that it is time to relax.

Breathe

Once you're sitting comfortably, turn your attention to the breath. Begin to take long, deep yogic breaths in and out of the nose, making full use of the lungs, from the belly, to the ribs and up to the collar bone. As explained in chapter 2, there are three parts to the full yogic breath – it begins deep down in the abdominal area, filling the ribs, up to the collar bone. When you breathe out the lungs will empty in the same order.

As you breathe in, you will feel your belly expanding and rising, and as you breathe out, you will feel the belly drop down and contract. Mindful breathing is a very effective way to calm the mind, stop the chattering monkeys and open the doors to peacefulness.

Mantras

One of the main stumbling blocks with learning to meditate is undoubtedly managing the many thoughts and concerns in our mind. So firstly, practise 'allowing' these thoughts, the more you try to resist them, the harder it will be to gain control over them. Secondly, practise using a mantra such as 'Om', which is the sound of the universe or 'So Ham' which is the sound of the breath. Breathe in and say in your mind, 'So', breathe out and say in your mind, 'Ham'. From Sanskrit this roughly translates to mean 'I am that I am' and it will help you to associate with something greater than your ego, which your mind thinks you are.

Another technique to focus the mind and improve concentration is to practise 'Tratak', where you focus on an object such as a candle's flame or a flower, without blinking, then close your eyes, allowing the image that you've been staring at to flood into your mind. (Place a candle at a safe distance in front of you.)

Although the mind will want to keep drifting away, you can bring it gently back by focusing on the sound and the motion of your breath, or on the object of your focus. You could repeat 'Who am I?' to help expand your conciousness once you have been meditating for some time. With practice, the amount of time when the mind is still and focused will gradually begin to increase.

'Mindful breathing is a very effective way to calm the mind, stop the chattering monkeys and to open the doors to peacefulness.'

Removing obstacles

Feeling too hot or cold and not feeling comfortable can be huge hinders to effective meditation, so make sure you give this your full attention before you begin. Check that you are warm enough, that your clothes are not digging into you and if you are finding a Lotus or cross-legged pose uncomfortable, change to sit in a chair.

The senses tend to agitate the mind as we are drawn towards certain desires, wants and needs, and are easily triggered by the sound of a song from the past, or the smell of someone's perfume. Learning to use sounds (such as the natural sound of the breath – 'So' on the inhalation and 'Ham' on the exhalation) or focusing on your chosen images or mantra is extremely useful.

Alternative Practices

As a preparation for meditation, you could try the following exercises, which will help improve concentration and reduce stress. Only when you have learnt to control your mind by managing your thoughts will true meditation follow.

Reading with awareness

Many of us will be familiar with the feeling of reading but not really reading and taking anything in, then having to go back a few pages to find out what's going on in the story! In today's multi-tasking, over-stimulated world, we almost need to 're-learn' how to concentrate on one thing at a time.So, next time you pick up a book, whatever kind of book it is, commit to being completely immersed in it for a chosen number of pages. This is an exercise in developing your awareness and improving your concentration skills – plus if it's a good book, it's time well spent!

Mindful walking

Go for a walk in the countryside, a park or along a beach and make a point of looking around you and emptying your mind of your thoughts about the day, or what else you need to do for the remainder of the day. Give yourself however long you can spare to walk in nature to focus your mind on the world around you. Again, this will improve your quality of life and your ability to meditate and live fully in each moment. Focus on the spine, the feet touching the ground, and practise breathing in from the earth, drawing its energy upwards to the crown of your head and back down again.

Stepping back

Practise standing back from your emotions on a daily basis, observing yourself dispassionately, as though watching someone else having those feelings. These thoughts and emotions will begin to lose their power over your concentration and you start to see that you are the true 'Master' of your mind.

Pranayama

The pranayama breathing exercises will also help to focus the mind ready for meditation, try the Anuloma Viloma exercise from chapter 8 and Kapalabhati from chapter 3. Both will help to reduce stress and bring you into the present moment.

Summing Up

Practising meditation will allow your thinking to become clearer and this will positively impact everything you do in life. Meditation creates space in the mind, and helps you to experience tranquillity, a relaxed and compassionate approach to life, improved sleep, healthy blood pressure, and better overall health.

Chapter Six

Yoga for Pregnancy

The experience of pregnancy and motherhood can be an extremely exciting as well as daunting period in a woman's life. Yoga is a very helpful support system during these times of change and is recognised by the National Childbirth Trust (NCT) as a relaxing and enormously beneficial therapy before, during and after pregnancy. Specialised breathing exercises help to reduce anxiety and gentle stretching helps prepare the mother physically, emotionally, mentally and spiritually for labour.

In this chapter Francoise Barbira Freedman – a medical anthropologist, author of many international-selling yoga and pregnancy books, mother of four, and the founder of the Birthlight Centre generously shares her wealth of personal and observational expertise in the niche area of pregnancy yoga.

Enjoy the journey

Rather than continuing with your regular yoga practice, recognise and surrender to an entirely new situation, a journey for you and your baby. The pregnancy modifications allow you to deepen your breathing and gain more from your practice, as you discover how to bond, breathe and move with another being growing inside you.

Yoga will also help you form a better connection and get to know your growing baby as the months progress. Prenatal yoga is not only beneficial for the mother-to-be, it is invaluable to the baby's future wellbeing as it helps set their neuro-endocrine responses and contributes to optimal brain development.

'Specialised breathing exercises help to reduce anxiety and gentle stretching helps prepare the mother physically, emotionally, mentally and spiritually for labour.'

Strong, toned pelvic floor muscles

With pregnancy yoga you will learn how to recognise, isolate and activate different muscle groups so that you can give birth lightly. The pelvic floor muscles are a range of muscles attached to your lower back and abdominal muscles, and they are vital for pregnancy and birth. These muscles need strengthening and toning so that all of the organs in the abdominal region can rest comfortably and in the correct place. You also need to prepare these muscles to become 'birthing muscles' and increase their elasticity.

'The pelvic floor muscles are a range of muscles attached to your lower back and abdominal muscles, and they are vital for your pregnancy and the birth.'

Take a deep breath

Using the breath efficiently helps you to relax, enjoy your pregnancy and give you more energy. But most importantly, it it is an invaluable resource to help you during the birth. When you breathe deeply and efficiently, you are not only nurturing yourself, but your baby too and prenatal bonding occurs naturally via this intravenous breathing. As you gain awareness you will see that your breathing is an invaluable tool connecting you physically, emotionally and spiritually with your body and baby.

The full yogic breath stretches all the way up from the pelvic muscles to the collar bone and it is vital to learn this skill and to understand the essence of the exhalation. In yoga, the inhalation is used to lengthen, stretch and to help you move into your asana; while the exhalation is used to help you go deeper, to release and let go. Understanding how to use your breath wisely is a wonderful and liberating skill to have and an essential skill during your pregnancy and birth.

Pregnancy yoga can alleviate pelvic pain, and help to prevent and relieve blockages in birth. The whole pelvic girdle is the core of yoga and in pregnancy you can only work on the abdominal muscles (which stretch to accommodate the expansion of the uterus) with the careful and controlled use of the breath.

Anxiety and depression are very common conditions during and after pregnancy, and both are increased by shallow breathing. By breathing deeply and thinking positively you learn to control anxiety, reduce depression and feel more in control. Meditation is also a precious and supportive skill, see chapter 5.

Getting aligned

You will need to learn how to get up and down from the floor (or the sofa) in such a way that the spine is in alignment so you protect and strengthen the lower back muscles which are key for childbirth.

Drawing on the ancient wisdom of yoga, you can adopt ways to move with ease as the pregnant body grows heavier. Yoga techniques teach you how to use your body in an aligned way so that you can roll over and go onto all fours, a movement which is conducive on a daily basis and will help promote a good birth.

'Drawing on the ancient wisdom of yoga, you can adopt ways to move with ease as the pregnant body grows heavier.'

The stages of pregnancy

If you follow the adapted yoga asanas then you can safely practise yoga throughout your pregnancy. According to Francoise the best yoga asanas for pregnant bodies are lots of spiralling flows and open twists, because it becomes very difficult to practise static poses without becoming tired.

Early pregnancy: one to 16 weeks

In these first few weeks it is good to slow down, do less on the physical side of yoga (even if you are very fit and are used to doing high impact exercise). Spend more time becoming aware of, and working with, your breath and your own ability to self-nurture and relax.

Mid-pregnancy: 16-34 weeks

This is generally considered to be the most enjoyable part of a woman's pregnancy, and as you will be feeling more balanced emotionally you can start building your physical strength and stamina. Do lots of standing and balancing poses and focus on creating good alignment of your spine to help your posture, prevent back and pelvic pain, and create room for your baby.

Late pregnancy: 34-40 weeks plus

Awareness of spinal alignment, toning the pelvic floor muscles and the special use of the breath is the key during the last term of your pregnancy. Yoga asanas, meditation, breathing, deep relaxation and visualisation practices will help prepare you mentally, spiritually and physically for the birth. Choose lots of seated asanas, using props like the bed, sofa and cushions to perform rotating hip-openers. Visualise yourself 'opening' and creating space for a light birth.

> 'The first point that I instil in pregnant mothers is that yoga during pregnancy needs to be adapted.'
>
> Francoise Barbira Freedman, yoga for pregnancy teacher and founder of Birthlight.

Birthlight

Birthlight is one of the pregnancy yoga pioneers in the UK. During the 1980s and 90s, before yoga became a mainstream and recommended therapy or exercise during pregnancy, it was the only place offering carefully adapted and developed classic yoga postures and breathing exercises for mothers and babies.

Francoise Barbira Freedman, founder of Birthlight, had practised hatha yoga with her father while growing up in France. However, when she became pregnant with her first child in the 1970s she felt that Iyengar yoga, which she had been practising, didn't allow sufficient 'flow' for her pregnant body. She was thus inspired to develop her own style of pregnancy yoga, which has its roots in hatha yoga, combined with flow and breath work, and the precision of Iyengar that she so loves. Here she explains more about yoga for pregnancy:

'I have spent over 30 years devising a programme of yoga which makes sense to pregnant women. The flow and the precise adaptation of the movement is what make these movements stand out. My goal is to pass on my knowledge and experiences that I had so that women have the ability to trust and surrender when they need to during the birthing process.

'In my teachings I believe that yoga can be done all the way through pregnancy and all of it is completely safe. The first point that I instil in pregnant mothers is that yoga during pregnancy needs to be adapted. Pregnancy is a completely new situation, a journey with your baby, and I don't believe we should impose rigid programmes which dictate for example, that at 30 weeks I can do this asana and at 40 weeks I must not do that asana.

'With a new life inside you, you are discovering how to breathe and how to move, and in this way you get to understand how your baby is growing inside you. I had two of my pregnancies when I was in the Amazon, and I had to work really hard, carrying heavy jars of water on my head, and doing tasks which required co-ordination of the breath and movements which were unfamiliar to me.

'I began to use my knowledge of yoga and rediscovered the flow of breath to cope with the greater stretching and effort. It felt wonderful to derive such tremendous energy, my baby felt strong and light and I felt agile and fit.

'When I returned to the UK I wanted to help other women have a better time during pregnancy, and have been dedicated to finding a way to reconcile birthing in hospitals, the skills I learnt in the Amazon, and the integration of breathing in movements that I had learned from my father.

'At Birthlight we propose three major periods which include the first three months after birth when the body is still coping with the changes. The important thing with yoga during pregnancy is to pass on this ancient art to the baby, so that the new life within you gets to benefit from your own practice.'

Practice

During pregnancy, it is a wonderful experience to be able to attend a pregnancy yoga class, as the teacher will go through various side effects and how to counter them with yoga. A good 'yoga for pregnancy book' can be the next best thing.

'During pregnancy, it is a wonderful experience to be able to attend a pregnancy yoga class, as the teacher will go through various side effects and how to counter them with yoga. A good 'yoga for pregnancy book' can be the next best thing.'

The following sequences are excerpts adapted from Francoise Barbira Freedman's book, *Yoga for Pregnancy, Birth and Beyond* (Dorling Kindersley), a highly recommended aide-memoire to guide you effortlessly through your pregnancy and beyond. Here, you can sample some of her recommendations.

! The mid- to late term suggestions should not be practised in the early stages. However, once you are in your mid- to late term you can also practise the early recommendations.

Relaxation

Make sure you spend at least five minutes in a relaxation position at the beginning and end of your session. Make the relaxation at the end longer so that your body can really reap the rewards of all the stretches and breathing that you have done. Use any of the poses below for your pregnancy yoga relaxation.

Front-facing Savasana

How

▨ Lie on your front on the mat with one knee bent to make room for your bump. Make a pillow with your arms and turn your face either to the right or left.

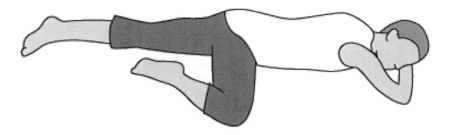

Child's pose (Balasana)

How

▨ Modify the typical Child's pose so that your knees are wide, making room for your baby bump.

Supine Butterfly

How

- Lie on your back and prop yourself up against lots of cushions in the Butterfly pose with knees wide and the soles of your feet together.

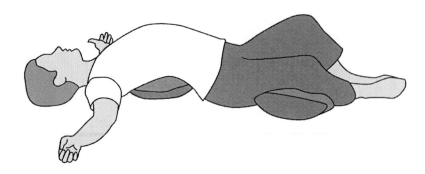

Early pregnancy

Basic pelvic alignment

This helps keep the pelvis symmetrical and prevents lower back pain which often arises from the pelvis being out of alignment.

How

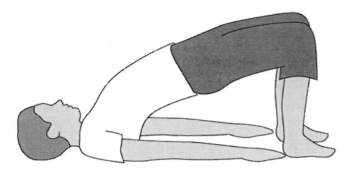

- Lie on your back with knees bent, feet flat on the floor and hip-width apart. Relax your back and let your spine be in full contact with the floor.

- As you breathe out, press the middle of your back onto the floor, your tailbone may lift slightly. Repeat these movements, then, pressing the palms of your hands onto the floor, lift your hips and gently sway your pelvis from side to side. Rest and breathe evenly.

- If you would like to take the stretch deeper, you can perform a slow Bridge: as you breathe in begin to lift your tailbone off the floor, and then exhale it back down. Next time you breathe in, raise yourself up another level from the floor then exhale back down again. Keep repeating until you have come up into full Bridge, and are resting on your shoulders. Your neck should feel supported, if in any pain come out of the pose slowly with an out breath, uncurling vertebrae by vertebrae

- The final stage is to breathe in, lift your hips off the floor and when you exhale let your left hip drop and raise your right hip. Repeat on the other side. Finally, exhale your back down onto the floor and breathe evenly, resting in the start position.

Sitting stretches

These help you to gain awareness of and enjoy a really good stretch of the muscle groups that allow you to walk and sit straight with your baby inside you.

How

▪ Sit on a firm seat with legs wide and knees level with your hips. Inhale and raise your right arm up, relaxing your neck and body. Exhale and stretch into your fingers and then release the arm down. Repeat with your left arm.

▪ Next, inhale and raise your right arm up and then over to the left side then down as you breathe out (be sure to keep your hips still). Repeat with the other arm.

▪ Widen your knees and take the stretch further down your spine. Imagine you are rolling a ball between your arms, rotating your torso as you slowly move your hands clockwise then anticlockwise.

▪ Then inhale and place the back of your left hand onto your right knee, and your right hand around your back against your left buttock, twist your upper body to the right side on an exhalation.

▪ Repeat on the other side.

Adapted Shoulderstand

Great for allowing blood circulation to flow to the pelvic area and the legs, and preventing varicose veins.

How

- Place a big cushion or beanbag up against a wall and lie down with your upper back and head on the floor, resting your hips/buttocks on the cushion and your feet up on the wall (keep knees bent). Relax your arms to the sides. Now, press your lower back into the cushion and stretch into your heels. Inhale and take your arms behind you to really open up your chest. Breathe evenly.

- If you feel comfortable, take a deep breath in to go into a Bridge variation; press your feet into the wall and raise your hips away from the cushion. Keep your arms at each side of the cushion. Exhale to lower your hips back down to the cushion.

- To complete the sequence, breathe in and bend your legs, drawing your knees to either side of your baby bump. Relax and breathe then let your legs rest fully on the cushion, arms at your sides.

Mid-pregnancy

Mountain (Tadasana)

Practising this asana will help to align your spine so that your posture is good during your pregnancy as your abdomen expands. At first, it is helpful to stand in front of a mirror to ensure proper alignment.

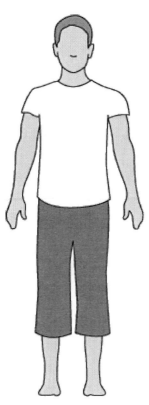

How

- Stand in Mountain pose with feet hip-width apart. Soften your knees then place your hands on your lower back to gently nudge your pelvis into position, dropping the tailbone downwards.

- Draw your shoulders back and down, drop your chin and lift your sternum (chest) to allow space for your baby bump.

- Ground your feet and breathe deeply in and out. To do a quick alignment check, place one hand on the base of your neck and the other on your lumbar curve (lower back). Adjust if you feel out of alignment and use the mirror for guidance.

Archer to Warrior

This sequence merges the classic postures of Archer and Warrior into a lovely flow to help mothers develop courage, power and concentration for birth.

How

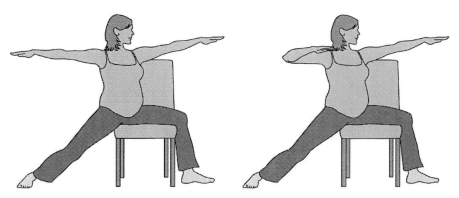

Archer

- Sit tall on a chair with knees wide apart and feet firmly grounded. Breathe deeply as you rest your hands on the chair seat.

- Straighten your right leg out to the side, and turn to your left, extending arms at shoulder height. Take your gaze to your left hand. Hold, and breathe.

- Let your left elbow drop onto your left thigh. Inhale and stretch your right arm up over your ear and turn your torso outwards as you breathe deeply, with a lovely open chest.

- Keep your lower body as it is and bring your torso back into an upright position, looking towards the left.

- Draw your right elbow backwards and keep your left arm stretched out at shoulder height towards the left side. Keep your gaze towards the fingers on your left hand in Archer pose. Breathe evenly.

Tall Warrior

- Inhale and raise both arms up overhead, bringing the palms together in Namaste Mudra. Look up at your hands, breathing deeply.

- Keep your back heel firmly grounded and your leg straight (N.B. the forward leg is bent). To complete this sequence, bring your arms down to your chest, and sit squarely once more on the chair as in the beginning. Breathe deeply, enjoying a renewed strength.

- Repeat the above on the left side.

Tree

'Tree is a marvellous asana to help you find balance – inside and out. You can use a chair to help support you.'

Tree is a marvellous asana to help you find balance – inside and out. You can use a chair to help support you.

How

- Rest your right knee on a chair with your hands in Namaste Mudra, and breathe evenly.

- Now place your right foot on the chair. Inhale and lift your left arm up, and look up at your hand, feeling a lovely stretch from your left heel to your fingers, letting your right hand rest loosely on your baby.

- Exhale and take your right foot off the chair and place the sole of your foot onto your left ankle or on the inner leg above the knee. Bring your hands to Namaste Mudra again, breathe deeply and bring your gaze forwards.

- If you feel stable, you can raise your foot higher up your left leg, on the inner thigh and take your arms out to the sides.

- Inhale and take the arms up overhead into Namaste Mudra, hold and breathe deeply then slowly release your arms and leg. Return to a wide Mountain with soft knees.

- Repeat on the left side.

Mid- to late pregnancy

From sitting to standing

Changing position requires special attention to ensure that you can keep your centre of gravity in the pelvis, protect your spine and maintain good posture.

How

- Once you feel unable to sit with a straight back without straining it, use a wall to align yourself. You can rest with the soles of your feet together, hips wide in Butterfly pose, with your back supported by the wall.

- To come out of this sitting position, slide your left foot close to your body and place your right foot in front of you. Take a breath in as you place your weight onto your hands. Exhale and slide your buttocks forward so that you are resting on your left heel.

- Next, bring your left hand forwards and your right knee on the floor and come onto all fours, bringing your weight slowly back towards your heels until your knees lift up completely and you are in a squat position. Walk your hands back. Your arms will be inside your knees.

- From this squat position, bring your hands into Namaste Mudra, and breathing in deeply, press your feet downwards and lift your spine up, uncurling vertebrae by vertebrae until you are finally standing up.

- When you are fully standing you can enjoy a further stretch, raising your arms up over your head and then letting them come back down to your sides.

Standing hip rolls

'As your birth date becomes closer, it is essential to focus on exercises which will help prepare you for labour, the hip roll is an excellent asana to reduce pain and encourage labour.

How

- Lean forwards against a wall, raising your arms quite high, pushing against it with your hands.

- As you breathe deeply, roll the hips in a circular motion, or swing them left to right, then right to left, in time with your breath.

Breathing for birth

Throughout pregnancy, practise using your breath to connect with your baby. As you prepare for the birth, chanting and sound vibrations will help free the voice and open the throat, while breathing out sounds during labour will help to ease the pain.

'As your birth date becomes closer, it is essential to focus on exercises which will help prepare you for labour, the hip roll is an excellent pose to reduce pain and encourage labour.'

How

- Relax on your bed, propped up with cushions, with your hands on your baby and your legs resting comfortably. Breathe in, then as you exhale make a loud, long sighing sound such as 'Aaah'.

- Make other sounds until you feel strong vibrations beneath your hands.

- Still relaxing on the bed, bend the knees, feet hip-width apart. Exhale as you make a deep grunting sound ('Huuh') to activate muscles of the perineum, then the sound of 'Hooh' to activate muscles around the uterus.

- Sit up straight to keep your throat open and as you breathe out, experiment with making different sounds, strengthening and lengthening the out breath as you do so.

Stretching for birth

Stretching is essential for reducing lower back pain and abdominal cramps, and this low rocking stretch will help develop better mobility around the tailbone and groin areas.

How

- Start in a kneeling position, on your heels, with your hands in front of you on the floor. Breathe deeply to release discomfort in the lower back.

- Come up onto your toes, lift one knee and softly rock your pelvis – sideways and back and forth. This helps your tailbone to relax.

- Alternatively, if you can squat comfortably with your heels on the floor and your back straight, rock in this position for deeper effects.

Relaxation

Always remember to finish your yoga session with a period of relaxation, use the modified poses mentioned at the beginning of the chapter during your pregnancy.

Summing Up

Set aside some time for yoga stretches and breathing every day during your pregnancy as this helps you to connect with your baby and brings you into the moment. Create a space that feels relaxing, comfortable and nurturing, with a few props for your practice, such as a blanket, chairs and cushions. You could also burn some incense, add an inspiring picture, some fresh flowers, a plant, and some relaxing music.

Chapter Seven

Yoga for Kids, Teachers and Parents

When babies lie on their backs, stretching out their legs, hips and arms, they are doing their own yoga. All these movements provide a lovely stretch across the front of the body, helping to build suppleness and, of course, enable body growth.

Yoga is a wonderful form of exercise for children – from toddlers up to teens. It is a great foundation and opportunity to introduce a healthy posture, co-ordination, breathing and essential life skills. A yoga session for children is all about fun, and can help them to chill out and relieve the pressures of homework, projects, after school activities and exams.

Yoga can also help children learn about their bodies and their intuition. In this chapter you'll learn some sample sessions which can be enjoyed with your children at home, or in the classroom.

'When babies lie on their backs, stretching out their legs, hips and arms, they are doing their own yoga.'

Fun time

Children don't want to take their yoga practice too seriously, so the basic rule is to keep the mood light and the emphasis on fun. Despite their obvious flexibility be mindful of their bodies' abilities, as their bones and muscles are still growing. Keep the sessions interactive and ask them questions, like how a particular asana makes them feel (tall as a tree, strong as a mountain etc.). Depending on the age of the children, you could use imaginative names for the postures, for example, Cobra becomes 'Sylvester the Snake' or Downward-facing Dog becomes 'Dusty the Dog' and so on.

Three key modifications for little ones

- Kids don't want to hold poses, they want to launch straight into them, so try to let go of precision and accuracy and just have fun, so that they come away from the session feeling good about themselves.

- Stimulate and expand their imagination with story-telling, the more creative and inspired, the better.

- Build their confidence using lots of positive reinforcements

'Children are exceptionally receptive to yoga; their bodies can quickly mould into, adjust, adapt and do all the challenging asanas which can take adults years to master.'

Varying the session for different ages

Children are exceptionally receptive to yoga; their bodies can quickly mould into, adjust, adapt and do all the challenging asanas which can take adults years to master. Take advantage of this, praise and nurture them for their ability and efforts, and above all have fun.

At all ages it is essential to be very encouraging, and let them know they are doing well. Make adjustment suggestions in a non-critical and positive way, avoiding 'no, not like that' statements and suggesting 'try doing it this way' instead.

- Children aged two to six love to role play; pretend to be something exciting like a fiery, roaring lion, a slithering snake, a barking dog, or a moaning cow.

- From seven onwards, children will be able to focus and understand more about yoga so turn it into a learning experience by introducing aspects of the yoga philosophy, probing them to answer questions such as: where did yoga originate? Or, which type of 'tree' are you? In which country is your 'mountain' located?

- From age 12 (sometimes younger, depending on the child) they might like to join in with an adult yoga session.

- Teenagers respond really well to yoga; their bodies are strong, fit and flexible. During adolescence, yoga can be a marvellous tool to help young people build individuality, develop a strong sense of who they are in the world, inner poise and self-confidence. They are often over-concerned with self-consciousness, peer comparison and wanting above all else to feel that they fit in and are liked, so make sure you boost their confidence and positively reinforce what they are doing. This is also a good time to challenge them to hold asanas for longer and do extra rounds of sun salutations (see chapter 3).

Practice

Below is a selection of fun yoga asanas for parents to try with their children, or for teachers to use in the classroom. The 20-30 minutes of physical asanas combined with 5-10 minutes of relaxation before and after the session will mentally, physically and emotionally refresh them.

Crocodile (Makrasana)

Crocodile is a wonderful resting and relaxation pose – especially good at the beginning of class as it helps children to let go of their day and helps calm their breathing and heart rate. It is also good for aligning the spine and refreshing all the chakras (the body's energy systems). Alternatively, you can use Savasana (see Before You Start).

'Crocodile is a wonderful resting and relaxation pose – especially good at the beginning of class as it helps children to let go of their day and helps to slow down the breathing and the heart rate.'

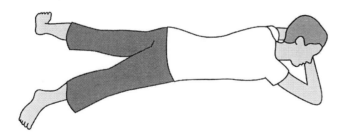

- Ask the children to lie on their fronts on their mat (or call it a 'magic carpet'), making a pillow with their hands to rest their foreheads on. Let their legs and feet go wide to the sides, with toes pointing out at a 45° angle.

- Get them to imagine their belly is like an inflatable beach ball, growing big as they breathe in and deflating as they breathe out. Spend about five minutes in Crocodile.

Downward-facing Dog (Adhomukha Svanasana)

Downward-facing Dog is one of the most widely recognised and popular yoga asanas and all of the benefits of this wonderful pose can be enjoyed by children, with some fun and imaginative modifications.

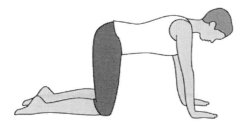

- Come out of the relaxation pose and go into Table pose.

- When in Table pose, tuck the toes under and on an in breath push the hips up into the air towards the ceiling.

- Breathe out and sink the heels back towards the mat while keeping hips high. Once settled into Downward-facing Dog, the children can begin barking and shaking their heads, pretending to sniff for food and scenting, if you want to make it more fun!

Need2Know

- Inhale, raise the right foot and lift the right leg up to the side (as if marking your territory!), exhale and place the right leg back down. Do the same on the left side.

Cobra (Bhujangasana)

Fun ways to use Cobra pose could include: letting the children make hissing sounds, wriggle and slither around the floor or getting into pairs and pretending one is a snake charmer!

How

- Get the children to lie on their fronts again, placing their hands at the sides of their bodies, next to the shoulders.
- As they breathe in they raise the head, neck and torso, just like a snake, and then breathe out to return back down again.

Tree (Vrkasana)

The Tree pose is excellent for developing balance, focus and improving their attention spans.

How

- Stand with feet parallel and hip-width apart. Put the weight into the left leg first – imagine the foot has roots growing out of the sole.

- Bend the right knee and slowly, gracefully lift up the right foot and place it on the inner leg, above the left knee.

- Keep eyes focused on something straight ahead to maintain balance. Inhale to bring the palms together into Namaste Mudra and breathe deeply.

- Exhale, release the arms and leg. Shake both legs like jelly and then do the same on the other side.

'Tree pose is excellent for developing balance, focus and improving their attention spans.'

Cat (Marjariasana) meets Cow

Use the Cat and Cow poses in a fun way – ask them to miaow and moo loudly when in each position!

How

- To begin with, kneel in Table pose (see Downward-facing Dog).

- As they exhale, arch their backs upwards so that they create a dome shape, tucking their chins into their chests, just like cats do when they enjoy a good old stretch. Miaow loudly!

- Then take a deep breath in and reverse the movement, slowly lowering the back from the base of the spine downwards, pushing the belly down towards the mat then lift the neck and head upwards – moo like a cow!

Games and playtime suggestions

Fairground roller coaster (all ages)

Make an imaginary visit to the fairground and take a ride on the roller coaster. As well as being great fun, the roller coaster ride provides important stretches, including forward bends, backbends and lateral twists of the spine – all essential moves in yoga!

How

- Sit on the floor with your legs out in front of you in a V shape. Then have another child sit in front and another behind and form a long line together with hands around each other's waists.

- Raise both arms then take them to the right, then left, then backwards, pretending you are riding on the roller coaster.

- Make lots of noise!

Walk in the countryside (great for toddlers and young yogis)

Take an imaginary walk in the countryside with 'Dusty the dog'!

How

- Ask the children to partner up, one child becomes the dog walker and the other the dog. The child acting as 'Dusty the dog' should be in Downward-facing Dog.

- Gently ask the dog walker to hold on to Dusty at the collar (gently hold their clothing) and let him walk around on all fours in Downward-facing Dog pose. Then swap over roles.

- Walk past a lake where you see lots of ducks. Both of you go into a squat, and place hands in front, one palm facing up, the other hand on top of that to emulate the beak and make duck sounds.

- Then impersonate the fish swimming in the lake with Fish pose – lie on your back, with legs straight out in front. Place arms underneath the bottom, palms facing down. Lift yourself up to lean on your elbows then exhale and open the chest and let your head drop down gently onto the mat behind.

- Walk past the fields and see the various animals – cow, cat and dog – doing each of the poses in turn and emulating the sounds they make.

- Rest under a shady tree one of you goes into Tree pose. then swap.

- Finally, give Dusty a treat – let him lie on his back with his legs in the air and tickle his tummy!

Visit the zoo (great for toddlers and young yogis)

Use an imaginary 'visit to the zoo' as a great excuse for children to practise the animal poses, enjoy!

How

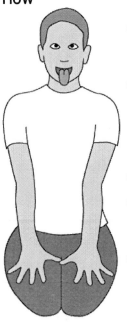

- First, visit the snake family in their pen. Children can slither across the floor in the Cobra pose making hissing sounds.

- Next, visit the lion pen and roar like a big, scary lion – to do Lion pose, kneel on your heels placing your hands on your knees, take a breath in. On the exhalation stick your tongue out as far as possible, widening your eyes and roaring loudly!

- Go to see the big crocodiles using Crocodile pose.

- Visit the bright pink flamingos – balance on one leg, lift the other leg behind you and stretch your arms out wide to the sides.

- See the cheeky monkeys in their enclosure – squat, letting your knees go wide, and swing your arms from side to side making monkey noises!

Summing Up

It is wonderful to see children go from super active and excited to deeply relaxed and refreshed after a session of yoga – physical asanas tire them out, the breath work and relaxation boosts oxygen levels and refreshes all the systems of the body. Plus, the games are great fun and a good opportunity for social interaction.

Yoga can also be a fantastic way of learning and increasing a level of appreciation and awareness for this amazing planet on which we reside – teach the younger children names of different trees as you go into Tree pose, the sounds and names of animals or different countries and landmarks as you take them on magic carpet journeys around the world on their yoga mats!

Chapter Eight

Yoga to Stay Young and Youthful

Since time began, people have searched for the Elixir of Youth – and with today's huge cosmetic surgery market and extensive range of anti-ageing products and treatments promising to reduce, remove and reverse the signs of ageing, the search goes on.

Although it wasn't designed with aesthetics or wrinkle-busting in mind, the tried and tested science of yoga can help keep us looking and feeling young and vital at every age. After all, ancient sages and yogis claim that ageing doesn't exist, rather that it is the result of intoxicating the body with alcohol, cigarettes, lack of sleep or exercise and stress - an interesting theory, and well worth considering.

Rewind and reverse it

Up until the age of 35 the regenerative (anabolic) cells are higher than the degenerative (catabolic) cells but around the mid- to late 30s the body begins to slow down its rejuvenating abilities. With the extreme demands of childbirth and of raising a family, women often succumb more quickly than men.

But, you can use yoga as a natural tool to defer and slow down ageing. Regular practise, a healthy diet and a positive mental attitude can help reverse these processes and help you stay younger looking and more flexible for longer.

There's just one catch – what you put in, you will get back!

'Many yoga asanas send oxygen and blood to the head, reducing oxygen-starved lines and wrinkles and putting a fresh glow into your face.'

Yoga is a carefully worked out system based on a great understanding of the human body and its functioning. The physical practice of yoga helps tone, lengthen and strengthen our bodies, improve posture and keep the spine lubricated and flexible. What's more, with regular practice we tend to be drawn towards a healthy and nutritious diet, which is also good for longevity.

Many yoga asanas send oxygen and blood to the head, reducing oxygen-starved lines and wrinkles and illuminating the face. The specialised breathing techniques help to oxygenate the mind and the body and the relaxation and meditation practices bring about a glow of inner peace, radiance and wellness.

Keeping in the flow

Looking young has a lot to do with blood flow, and according to the ancient yogis, improving this is the holy grail of youthfulness and vitality. Blood brings oxygen, sugar, vitamins and other nutrients to the brain and removes carbon dioxide and other waste products but the flow of blood decreases over time, especially to the brain. Drinking too much coffee or tea, smoking and being dehydrated are three key factors which exacerbate ageing as they constrict the flow of blood - as does stress, lack of exercise and sleep - all things many of us can relate to today.

However, once you begin practising and realise how good yoga can make you feel, you may find you do not want or need to drink coffee at all; and your desire to smoke could also simply disappear as you cleanse and exercise your lungs in the pranayama exercises.

Eating to stay young

Many yogis today choose to eat a vegetarian diet as this is in alignment with the philosophy of yoga and non-violence, known as Ahimsa in Patanjali's Yoga Sutras (see page 25). As well as being simple, wholesome and natural, the vegetarian diet honours the effect that food has on the body and on the mind, the closer our food is to the source of energy (the sun), the better the source of positive energy. However, not everyone who practises yoga follows a vegetarian diet, and it's a personal choice. Moderation is the key to a healthy diet.

Fasting and inner cleansing

We are constantly absorbing toxins from the environment, our diet and lifestyles, which can leave us vulnerable to a range of disorders. Although the human body has the natural mechanism to detoxify itself, it could certainly use a little assistance.

Many of us today overeat, over-indulge, eat too late in the day, drown rich food with wine, and drink too much coffee to cope with a fast-paced, demanding lifestyle. So, keeping the body clean on the inside through fasting and inner cleansing is really important.

The colon is one of the most important organs of the body, much of the body's immunity and defence systems are located here and, if overworked and congested, the body and mind will also feel overworked and congested. This has a very ageing effect on the mind, body and soul.

Fasting will take some pressure off your colon and is a wonderful way to put the sparkle back into your face and eyes, and make your skin glow like a teenager's. Physically, fasting is considered to be a cure-all for many different problems (the body does it naturally when it is ill or in pain). Cleansing through fasting improves your metabolic rate, helps you feel invigorated, motivated and vital by eliminating poisons, and allowing other organs, such as the liver and kidneys, a chance to rest and renew. Mentally, fasting clears the mind, improves focus and concentration.

Make sure you choose a quiet time to fast, when you will have few demands. Drink only fruit or vegetable juices and water for one to two days, and break the fast gently, moving on to steamed vegetables, fruit with natural yoghurt and introducing other food such as brown rice, porridge and nuts very slowly.

! You should check with your GP that it is safe for you to fast, this will not be an option for everyone.

! Fasting should never be practised during pregnancy.

Yoga practice for staying young

Anuloma Viloma (alternate nostril breathing)

The practice of regular pranayama is thought to purify the bloodstream, improve the quality of sleep, advance the power of the mind and slow down old age. The Anuloma Viloma breathing exercise increases oxygen to the brain, clears the mind and cleanses the nasal passages. It also balances the right and left hemispheres of the brain and the catabolic (degeneration) and anabolic (regeneration) rates, making it an excellent exercise to practise for anti-ageing purposes!

'The practice of regular pranayama is thought to purify the bloodstream, improve the quality of sleep, advance the power of the mind and slow down old age.'

How

- Sit comfortably on the floor in a cross-legged or Lotus variation with a pillow or cushion beneath you so that your back is straight and supported. Alternatively sit upright in a chair.

Vishnu Mudra

- Place your left hand into Chin Mudra (index finger and thumb lightly touching) then place your right hand into Vishnu Mudra. (See diagram.)

- Take an in breath then place your thumb over your right nostril, and breathe out of your opposite nostril (on the left side). Then breathe in through the left side, close this side with your ring finger so that both nostrils are closed just for a few beats, then remove your thumb from your right nostril so that you are exhaling out of the opposite nostril.

- When you feel you have completely exhaled, breathe in through your right nostril, and again close both nostrils for a few beats before proceeding to breathe out of the opposite nostril.

- Beginners can continue for three to six rounds but should stop if any dizzy feelings or nausea occur. Gradually increase the number of rounds and the amount of time between inhalation and exhalation.

- ! Do not retain the breath in this practice if you have high blood pressure.

- ! Do not practise if you have a cold/blocked nose.

Inversions

Shoulderstand, Half Shoulderstand and Headstand are excellent asanas to fight the forces of gravity which cause sagging and organs to be displaced. Known as the 'king' (Headstand) and 'queen' (Shoulderstand) of asanas these inverted poses allow blood to drain from the legs and around the entire body and face, feeding tissues and skin which is starved of blood and poor circulation. As a result they are considered to be the ultimate anti-ageing asanas.

Both Headstand and Shoulderstand are quite advanced postures and should only be practised by experienced yogis, preferably after warming up with some sun salutations. Beginners should seek some tuition from a yoga instructor before attempting these poses, or follow the adapted Shoulderstand, as shown in chapter 6.

'Inversions improve circulation and send oxygen and blood to tired tissues.'

A suitable alternative for beginners (and for experienced yogis not wanting to do an inversion) is the Child's pose (Balasana), a resting posture which enables oxygen and blood to replenish tired tissues (explained in Before You Start).

! Do not practise inversions if you have high blood pressure, a history of strokes, a heart condition or spinal problems, such as a neck or back injury.

! Inversions are not recommended during menstruation as it is thought to interfere with the flow of energy – but this is a decision for the individual.

! Inversions are not recommended during pregnancy (see chapter 6 for pregnancy modifications).

Half Shoulderstand and Shoulderstand (Ardha Sarvangasana and Sarvangasana)

It is vital that you warm-up before attempting the inverted poses with at least three to six rounds of sun salutations.

How

- Lie on your back with bent knees and walk your feet up towards your hips.

- Place your hands face down at the side of your hips, you will use these as brakes to balance coming in and out of the pose.

- Lift your legs up into the air, at an angle of around 30-45°. Then, taking a deep breath in and pressing down on your hands, raise your hips off the mat and direct your legs upwards gradually, walking your hands up your back so you are resting on your shoulders. As the weight of your body is on your shoulders you shouldn't feel any pain in your neck or anywhere else. Come out of this pose immediately by following the instructions below if you do. Breathe evenly.

- Don't worry about how far your legs go up – you will achieve the same benefits as the blood flows from your legs towards your heart.

- Follow the same instructions for full Shoulderstand with your legs at an angle of 90°.

- To come out of the pose, place your hands beside your hips for control, engage your abdominal muscles and gently unfold vertebrae by vertebrae until your back is completely on the mat. Keep your knees bent as you place your feet on the floor, then extend your legs in front, and rest in Savasana for several breaths.

Headstand (Sirsasana)

It is recommended that you ask a qualified yoga teacher to instruct you into Headstand. This pose should only be practised if you are experienced, and it's recommended that you warm-up first with three to six rounds of sun salutations, followed by Child's pose.

How

- Start in Child's pose, sit up on your heels and place each hand on the opposite elbow then place them down onto the floor in front of you. Extend your hands forward, interlacing your fingers to form a tripod shape and place the crown of your head inside this triangular shape. This is your head support.

- Raise your hips and straighten your legs behind you. Engage your core muscles (abdominals, gluts and pelvic floor) and slowly walk your feet towards your head. When you can walk no further, bend your knees towards your chest, and bring your heels up to your buttocks. This is Half Headstand – rest here for up to a minute then come back down.

- If you are going to continue to Headstand, you should slowly straighten your back and hips so that the bent knees are pointing upwards.

- Finally, when you feel fully balanced, you can straighten your legs so your feet go up towards the ceiling. Breathe deeply.

- Return to Half Headstand to come out of the pose, straightening your legs behind you, then resting in Child's pose, followed by Savasana.

! Headstand should not be practised if you have eye conditions such as glaucoma or a detached retina.

! Do not practise inversions if you have high blood pressure, have a history of strokes, a heart condition or spinal problems, such as a neck or back injury.

! Inversions are not recommended during menstruation as it is thought to interfere with the flow of energy – but this is a decision for the individual.

! Inversions are not recommended during pregnancy (see Chapter 6 for pregnancy modifications).

Forward Bend (Paschimotasanasana)

The Forward Bend is an excellent asana for the entire body and is a fabulous preventative and maintenance asana, helping to relieve the menopause, PMS, diabetes, insomnia, stress, depression and so much more. Forward Bends are also great for letting go of unhealthy habits and addictions - great if you are beginning a new diet or healthy lifestyle change!

How

- To do a seated Forward Bend, sit with your legs straight out in front of you, lengthening from the base of your spine to the crown of your head.

- Inhale and reach your arms up over your head, then exhale and fold forwards from your hips, reaching your arms down towards your knees.

- Keep repeating the in breath to reach upwards and the out breath to extend and sink downwards until you feel you have reached your 'maximum', or edge, and hold, breathing evenly.

- You can enhance the psychic benefits of this pose by affirming: 'I let go with ease.'

- To do this asana standing up, follow a similar process. Stand tall in Tadasana (Mountain pose), then breathe in, lifting your arms straight overhead and exhale as you fold down from the pelvis, reaching forwards with a straight back first, before relaxing your head and neck down and taking hold of your ankles, feet or toes.

! Fold from the hips and pelvis, not from the belly. Think less about how far down you can go, but more about lengthening and strengthening the back.

! Do not practise this asana if you have a slipped disc, or sciatica.

! If you have knee/hip problems practise with caution.

Camel (Ustrasana)

The Camel (standing or kneeling) is an excellent yoga asana for overall health and wellbeing and for anti-ageing. You can do this asana standing or kneeling.

How

▪ Kneel on your mat with legs hip-width apart and place your hands on your lower back for support.

▪ Inhale and slowly bend backwards. Very mindfully, let your head go back first, followed by your shoulders, your chest and your lower back. Breathe out, and continue taking steady breaths.

▪ Inhale to come out of the pose, contracting your abdomen and lifting yourself up very gently and slowly.

▪ To do standing camel, place your feet hip-width apart and your hands on your lower back as above. Roll your shoulders back, moving the shoulder blades towards each other. Push your pelvis forwards and inhale to lift your chest and arch your upper back. Breathe evenly. Inhale to come up gently.

! Do not practise Camel if you have high or low blood pressure, get migraines, or have serious lower back or neck problems.

Triangle (Trikonasana)

As well as doing Forward Bend and Camel asanas in equal amounts, rotating the spine laterally is also integral to achieving a nice fluid and mobile spine. Regular practice of the Triangle will help keep the entire gastrointestinal system in good order, which will benefit your complexion.

How

- Stand with your feet apart and parallel, roughly the length of two times your shoulders. Bring your left foot 90° to the left side and turn your right heel 45° to the right side.

- Inhale and raise your right arm up towards the ceiling. Exhale and bend the trunk of the body over your left side, turn your head to look up at your right thumb. Your left arm will slide down your leg, towards your foot. Try to keep your hips, body and arm in one straight line - keeping the crown of the head in alignment with your spine.

- Inhale, bend your knee to lift up and out of the pose, and exhale to go back down into it. Then change sides. It can be helpful to practise this asana with your back flat against a wall, to ensure you do not lean forwards or backwards with the hips.

! If you have a back, hip or knee injury you should practise Triangle cautiously, coming out of the pose immediately if you feel any discomfort or pain.

! If you have neck pain or high blood pressure, keep the head turned downwards, and keep the raised arm down on the hip if you have a heart condition.

'Regular practice of the Triangle will help keep the entire gastrointestinal system in good order.'

Summing Up

Old age cannot be avoided but it can be deferred and you can choose to age gracefully. There is great beauty in a person whose face is lit up by acceptance, self-love, compassion, wisdom and peacefulness. Yoga is a safe method to help you stay young and vital, through the physical asanas, regular relaxation, pranayama, good diet, positive thinking and meditation.

Chapter Nine

Senior Yoga

You can start doing yoga at any age in your life but, according to yoga philosophy, once you have reached your 40s, you are more receptive and better mentally prepared to embrace all that yoga is and it is never too late to begin!

If you have been doing yoga for some time, then you will be able to continue with your regular practise well into your 60s and 70s and this chapter is designed for late-starting yogis who will see that with the cunning use of chairs, walls and other props yoga, meditation and relaxation can be adapted to suit all ages. The body has incredible regenerative abilities and with regular practice you will be amazed at what you can achieve. Here are some of the benefits:

- The retirement years can be the perfect opportunity to pursue new interests and make new friends. Yoga can be a wonderful tool for helping with low motivation and depression, often brought on by loneliness – it is a non-competitive and non-aggressive form of exercise and a great activity to do with other people.

- It can be a vicious circle when we age because as we become prone to aches and pains we move less and this lack of movement leaves us vulnerable to other illnesses and problems. Yoga can help to reduce and slow down the ageing process, and some of the conditions that start later in life which are exacerbated by a sedentary lifestyle.

- A lack of exercise can affect our quality of sleep and the body's circulation becomes slower without movement. Efficient breathing is therefore all the more important as we get older to help blood and oxygen circulate around the body.

- Yoga can help you gain a better sense of balance as some of the poses work directly on strengthening our mental, as well as our physical, ability to balance, which will help prevent falls.

'The body has incredible regenerative abilities and with regular practice you will be amazed at what you can achieve.'

■ Don't worry if your mobility is impaired there is still plenty you can do while seated. Otherwise, you can use the wall and chairs for support. If your body feels too stiff in the morning, do the physical exercises in the afternoon when your body is likely to feel more supple.

Yogic breathing

We sleep better after exercising, and of course, our circulation improves with movement, but if you're too tired, unwell or physically unable to do any exercises, try some refreshing yogic breathing instead.

How

■ Sitting down on a chair, place both feet flat on the ground and sit tall – imagine your spine lengthening from the base to the crown of your head. Place your arms loosely by your sides, get comfortable and cover yourself with a warm blanket if you wish.

■ Breathe in through your nose and exhale deeply out of your mouth, making a sighing sound. Normally in yoga, the breath is in and out of the nose but an exhalation out of the mouth really helps to let go. Repeat a few times.

■ Closing your eyes, begin the three-stage yogic breath. Firstly, breathe in through your nose, you will feel the movement starting low down in your abdomen. The breath expands in your belly, then rises up to your chest, expanding the ribs, finally rising to the shoulders and collar bone.

■ As you exhale out of your nose feel your belly emptying first, then your ribs and then your upper chest. To focus the mind, breathe in and count 1-2-3 then breathe out counting 3-2-1.

As an alternative, you could also try the Anuloma Viloma breathing technique – see chapter 8, an excellent anti-ageing exercise, which fllushes the brain with fresh oxygen and is believed to keep the mind lively and alert.

Feel-good visualisation

Yoga is much more than just physical and the power of the mind can help us change our thought patterns and moods to positive and helpful ones. Yogis visualise themselves in certain asanas before actually doing them. See yourself doing the asanas listed below in your mind's eye beforehand to help support your body's flexibility and movement.

To relax your mind and refresh the nervous and endocrine systems, think of a really calming scene, for example, somewhere you went on holiday or a place you've visited and felt contentment. Picture the scene in great detail, imagine you are there experiencing the sights and sounds, the birds, smell of flowers or freshly mown grass, the ocean. In your mind, repeat to yourself over and over 'I feel, strong, relaxed and well'. After 5-10 minutes, gently open your eyes and move gently.

The meditation techniques mentioned in chapter 5 are also highly recommended to improve concentration, memory, creativity and harmony.

Practice

Seated Spinal Twist

Twists help with sluggish digestion, compressed breathing and they feel good from the inside out because blood and toxins are squeezed out when we twist, and new blood and oxygen flow in on the release.

How

- Sitting down on a chair, place both feet flat on the ground and sit tall. Take a deep breath in, lifting and lengthening your spine from the base to the crown of your head.

- Bring your left hand across your right leg and your right arm onto the side of the chair for support.

- With a deep exhalation, slowly begin to twist your body towards the right side from the lower back, then the middle back, the upper back, and finally the neck and head. Do not force the movement.

- Inhale to return to centre then repeat on the other side.

! Do not practise if you have a back, neck or spine injury.

! Do not practise twists late at night - they are very stimulating!

Seated Forward Bend and Leg Lift

The Forward Bend massages all of the internal organs and is particularly beneficial for diabetes patients as it helps to regulate pancreas function. It also nourishes the digestive system, alleviating constipation and keeping you 'regular'.

How

- Breathe in, lift and lengthen your back from the base of your spine then exhale and fold forwards towards your knees and feet. Don't worry about how far you can bend, focus more on keeping your back as straight as possible and letting the movement come from your hips, rather than simply rounding the middle of your back. Take a few deep breaths here.

- Still in Forward Bend, take a breath in and see if you can lift your right leg up off the floor by taking hold of your right foot and straightening the back of your leg to stretch out your hamstrings. Only raise your leg as far as feels comfortable for you, the other leg, with your foot on the floor, will help give you balance. This exercise is more advanced so don't worry if it isn't possible to raise your leg, keep working on building flexibility by practising the forward bend and the other suggested exercises, and work towards this goal.

▨ Exhale and bend your knee, placing your foot back on the floor, repeat on the other side.

❗ Do not practise this asana if you have a slipped disc or sciatica.

❗ If you have knee/hip problems practise with caution.

Seated Backbend and Leg Lift

Backbends are really powerful stretches that help increase vitality and circulation to flow freely to the heart and lungs.

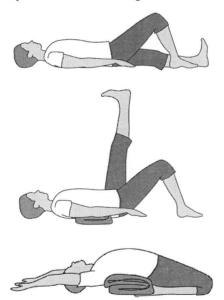

'Backbends are really powerful stretches that help increase vitality and circulation to flow freely to the heart and lungs.'

How

▨ Take a number of large cushions or folded blankets and put them to one side. Lie down on your back and bend your knees so that the soles of your feet are on the floor.

- Inhale and tilt up your tailbone then exhale and place it back down on the floor. Keep your back nice and flat on the floor then take another breath in and raise your right leg (the leg may be bent, but work towards straightening it to stretch the hamstrings), keeping your left knee bent and left foot flat on the floor.

- Work towards raising your right leg up to a 45° then a 90° angle, gently breathing in and out as you do so – use the exhalation to deepen the movement and the inhalation to stretch upwards. Do the same on the opposite leg.

- Now place the cushions or blankets behind you, underneath your lower back, and stretch both legs out in front. Breathe in and lift your arms up over your head. The cushions help open your chest so you can breathe more easily and increase flexibility in the spine and back muscles. The more cushions you have, the more you can lift up and expand the chest area and enjoy a few moments of deep efficient breathing.

! Do not practice the backbend if you have had recent abdominal surgery.

! Do not practice the backbend if you have a peptic ulcer, hernia, an over-active thyroid or back muscle spasms.

Standing Spinal Twist

This exercise will help to strengthen your leg muscles, and you get all the benefits of a twist, from the inside out.

How

- Standing up tall, cross your legs and stretch your arms out to your sides at shoulder height.

- Inhale and twist in the direction of your front leg and turn to look at your back arm.

- Release on an out breath, repeating on the other side.

! Do not practise twists if you have a back, neck or spine injury - seek supervision from an experienced teacher.

! Twists are re-energising so don't practise late at night.

Hip Hug and Tree (Vrkasana)

The Tree pose helps to strengthen the legs, improve balance and mental focus; and the hip-opening exercise is good preparation, stretching and relieving tightness in the hip joints and promoting mobility. A wall will help you keep your balance.

How

- Standing on your feet with a wall behind you, put the weight into your left leg.

- Breathe in and bend your right leg, lifting your knee upwards and wrapping your arms around it. Take a few deep breaths, then exhale, release, shake the legs and change sides.

- To go into Tree pose, bend your right knee and slowly lift up your right foot and place it on your left ankle, or on your inner leg above your left knee, depending on the flexibility in your hip joint is. Keep pressing your back into the wall to keep your balance.

- Breathe out. Raise both your arms to your heart in Namaste Mudra and hold, breathing deeply.

- Release, shake your legs out and change sides.

  ! Do not practise the hips hugs or Tree pose if you have hip/knee injuries or you have had replacement surgery (hip or knee).

Summing Up

This chapter demonstrates that you don't need to be young in order to practise yoga. By simply sitting in your favourite chair, or using a wall or some cushions, you can still enjoy the many benefits of yoga.

The physical asanas will increase your energy and mood while breathing exercises and meditation will help keep your mind alert and receptive so you can enjoy your golden years to the full.

In the senior years it's all about adapting to your body's needs and accepting its capabilities, without judgement.

Some days, any physical practise will be too much. On those occasions, try some breathing, meditation or visualisation techniques instead and return to the physical asanas when you have more energy.

Help List

Be Mindful

www.bemindful.co.uk
A website dedicated to meditation techniques to reduce stress and boost attention and concentration.

Birthlight

Tel: 01223 362288
francoise@birthlight.com
www.birthlight.com
Birthlight is an educational charity which draws on the parenting style of Amazonian forest people and yoga. It was founded by Francoise Barbira Freedman who has created simple, modified exercises and relaxation techniques to assist in pregnancy, birth and beyond.

British Autogenic Society

The Royal London Homoeopathic Hospital, Great Ormond Street, London, WC1N 3HR
Tel: 020 7391 8908
www.autogenic-therapy.org.uk
A professional and educational organisation offering information about research-based relaxation technique, where it came from, who can benefit and where to learn it.

British Wheel of Yoga

BWY Central Office, 25 Jermyn Street, Sleaford, Lincolnshire, NG34 7RU
Tel: 01529 306851
Fax: 01529 303233
www.bwy.org.uk
Provides details about yoga courses, training, teachers and workshops.

Dru Worldwide

Snowdonia Mountain Lodge, Nant Ffrancon, Bethesda, Bangor, LL57 3LX
Tel: 01248 602900
www.druworldwide.com
Dru yoga is a therapeutic flowing style of yoga which is especially beneficial for relieving back pain. To find out more visit the website.

Iyengar Yoga

IYA (UK), PO Box 4730, Sheffield, S8 2HE
Tel: 07510 326997
www.iyengaryoga.org.uk
The official website for Iyengar yoga in the UK. Provides information for students and teachers and has a search facility for teachers.

London Meditation Centre

www.london-meditationcentre.com
A centre offering Vedic meditation courses and workshops, based in London. Contact them via their website.

Sarah Dawson (Karmiyoga)

www.karmiyoga.com
Author, Sarah Dawson's website gives details about her yoga classes, courses and retreats.

Sivananda Yoga Vedanta Centre

51 Felsham Road, London, SW15 1AZ
Tel: 0208 780 0160
London@sivananda.org
www.sivananda.org
Provides information about courses, workshops and how yoga can help achieve health and calm in your life.

Transcendental Meditation (TM)

www.t-m.org.uk
Tel: 01695 51213
Offers courses, workshops and information about TM, which was founded by
Maharishi Mahesh Yogi.

Yoga Abode

www.yoga-abode.com
An online UK-based yoga magazine site, find information on yoga, wellbeing
and lifestyle.

Yoga Journal

www.yogajournal.com
Yoga Journal is a US-based magazine with information on poses, meditation
and all things yoga.

Yoga Magazine

www.yogamagazine.co.uk
A UK-based magazine with information on yoga, lifestyle, news and reviews.

Book List

Pilates – The Essential Guide
By Annabel Kent, Need2Know, Peterborough, 2010.

The Sivananda Companion to Yoga
By Swami Vishnu-Devanandra, Simon & Schuster, London, 2000.

Yoga for Pregnancy, Birth and Beyond
By Francoise Barbira Freedman, Dorling Kindersley, London, 2004.

Dru Yoga, Stillness in Motion
By Annie Jones, Anita Goswami and Chris Barrington

YogaKids, Educating the Whole Child Through Yoga
by Marsha Wenig

    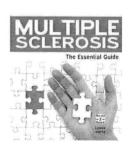